TRANSPORTATION ISSUES, POLICIES AND R&D

AF764371

THE HIGHWAY TRUST FUND

FINANCIAL CONDITION AND USE OF FUNDS

TRANSPORTATION ISSUES, POLICIES AND R&D

THE HIGHWAY TRUST FUND

FINANCIAL CONDITION AND USE OF FUNDS

JONATHAN CAULFIELD
EDITOR

NOVINKA
New York

Copyright © 2015 by Nova Science Publishers, Inc.

All rights reserved. No part of this book may be reproduced, stored in a retrieval system or transmitted in any form or by any means: electronic, electrostatic, magnetic, tape, mechanical photocopying, recording or otherwise without the written permission of the Publisher.

For permission to use material from this book please contact us:
nova.main@novapublishers.com

NOTICE TO THE READER

The Publisher has taken reasonable care in the preparation of this book, but makes no expressed or implied warranty of any kind and assumes no responsibility for any errors or omissions. No liability is assumed for incidental or consequential damages in connection with or arising out of information contained in this book. The Publisher shall not be liable for any special, consequential, or exemplary damages resulting, in whole or in part, from the readers' use of, or reliance upon, this material. Any parts of this book based on government reports are so indicated and copyright is claimed for those parts to the extent applicable to compilations of such works.

Independent verification should be sought for any data, advice or recommendations contained in this book. In addition, no responsibility is assumed by the publisher for any injury and/or damage to persons or property arising from any methods, products, instructions, ideas or otherwise contained in this publication.

This publication is designed to provide accurate and authoritative information with regard to the subject matter covered herein. It is sold with the clear understanding that the Publisher is not engaged in rendering legal or any other professional services. If legal or any other expert assistance is required, the services of a competent person should be sought. FROM A DECLARATION OF PARTICIPANTS JOINTLY ADOPTED BY A COMMITTEE OF THE AMERICAN BAR ASSOCIATION AND A COMMITTEE OF PUBLISHERS.

Additional color graphics may be available in the e-book version of this book.

LIBRARY OF CONGRESS CATALOGING-IN-PUBLICATION DATA

ISBN: 978-1-63482-012-7

Published by Nova Science Publishers, Inc. † New York

CONTENTS

Preface		**vii**
Chapter 1	The Status of the Highway Trust Fund and Options for Financing Highway Spending. Testimony of Joseph Kile, Assistant Director for Microeconomic Studies, Congressional Budget Office. Hearing on "New Routes for Funding and Financing Highways and Transit"	**1**
Chapter 2	Projections of Highway Trust Fund Accounts under CBO's August 2014 Baseline *Congressional Budget Office*	**33**
Chapter 3	Highway Trust Fund: DOT Has Opportunities to Improve Tracking and Reporting of Highway Spending *United States Government Accountability Office*	**35**
Index		**75**

PREFACE

In recent years, dedicated revenues to the Highway Trust Fund have been eroding, resulting in fewer resources to fund surface transportation projects and requiring, between 2008 and 2014, transfers of over $50 billion in general revenues. This book reviews how Highway Trust Fund monies are being used to help ensure that sound choices and investment decisions about future funding are made. The book examines what is known about the types of projects, activities, and federal administrative functions and expenses supported by the Department of Transportation (DOT) using Highway Trust Fund monies in fiscal year 2013.

Chapter 1 – Testimony of Joseph Kile, Assistant Director for Microeconomic Studies, Congressional Budget Office.

Chapter 2 – This is an edited, reformatted and augmented version of a document issued by the CBO, August 27, 2014

Chapter 3 – In recent years, dedicated revenues to the Highway Trust Fund have been eroding, resulting in fewer resources to fund surface transportation projects and requiring, between 2008 and 2014, transfers of over $50 billion in general revenues.

Four operating administrations within DOT—FHWA, FTA, NHTSA, and FMCSA—receive funding from the Highway Trust Fund for programs administered by these agencies, and FHWA receives the largest share (81 percent of the agency's authorizations in fiscal year 2013).

GAO was asked to review how Highway Trust Fund monies are being used to help ensure that sound choices and investment decisions about future funding are made. This report examines what is known about the types of projects, activities, and federal administrative functions and expenses supported by DOT using Highway Trust Fund monies in fiscal year 2013.

TRANSPORTATION ISSUES, POLICIES AND R&D

Additional books in this series can be found on Nova's website under the Series tab.

Additional e-books in this series can be found on Nova's website under the e-book tab.

To address this request, GAO obtained and analyzed fiscal year 2013 federal obligation data from DOT's operating administrations, reviewed relevant documentation, and interviewed FHWA, FTA, FMCSA, NHTSA, and DOT officials.

In: The Highway Trust Fund
Editor: Jonathan Caulfield
ISBN: 978-1-63482-012-7
© 2015 Nova Science Publishers, Inc.

Chapter 1

THE STATUS OF THE HIGHWAY TRUST FUND AND OPTIONS FOR FINANCING HIGHWAY SPENDING. TESTIMONY OF JOSEPH KILE, ASSISTANT DIRECTOR FOR MICROECONOMIC STUDIES, CONGRESSIONAL BUDGET OFFICE. HEARING ON "NEW ROUTES FOR FUNDING AND FINANCING HIGHWAYS AND TRANSIT"*

NOTES

Numbers in the text and tables may not add up to totals because of rounding.

Unless otherwise indicated, all years are federal fiscal years, which run from October 1 to September 30.

* This is an edited, reformatted and augmented version of testimony presented May 6, 2014 before the Senate Committee on Finance. The testimony was prepared by Sarah Puro and Chad Shirley with contributions from additional CBO staff.

Chairman Wyden, Senator Hatch, and Members of the Committee, thank you for the invitation to testify on issues related to the status of the Highway Trust Fund and on options for financing highway improvements and construction.

SUMMARY

In 2013, governments at various levels spent $156 billion to build, operate, and maintain highways, and they spent $60 billion on mass transit systems. For both types of infrastructure, most of that spending was by state and local governments; about one-quarter of that total came from the federal government, mostly through the Highway Trust Fund. For several decades, the trust fund's balances were stable or growing, but more recently, annual spending for highways and transit has exceeded the amounts credited to the trust fund from taxes collected on gasoline, diesel fuel, and other transportation-related products and activities. Since 2008, in fact, lawmakers have transferred $54 billion from the U.S. Treasury's general fund to the Highway Trust Fund so that the trust fund's obligations could be met in a timely manner.

Moreover, with its current revenue sources, the Highway Trust Fund cannot support spending at the current rate. The Congressional Budget Office (CBO) estimates that, at the end of fiscal year 2014, the balance in the trust fund's highway account will fall to about $2 billion and the balance in its transit account will be only $1 billion. Spending for highways and transit will be $45 billion and $8 billion, respectively. By comparison, revenues collected for those purposes are projected to be $33 billion and $5 billion, respectively. The Department of Transportation (DOT) has indicated that it will probably need to delay payments to states at some point during the summer of 2014 in order to keep the fund's balance above zero, as required by law. Then, if nothing changes, the trust fund's balance will be insufficient to meet all of its obligations in fiscal year 2015, and it will incur steadily accumulating shortfalls in subsequent years. If lawmakers do not take action, all of the receipts credited to the fund in 2015 would be needed to meet obligations made before that year; none would be available to cover any new commitments that would be made in 2015.

Several options (or combinations of those options) could be pursued to address projected shortfalls in the Highway Trust Fund:

- *Spending on highways and transit could be reduced.* If lawmakers chose to address the projected shortfalls solely by cutting spending, no new obligations from the fund's highway account or its transit account could be made in fiscal year 2015; that would also be the case for the transit account in fiscal year 2016. Over the 2015–2024 period, the highway account would see a decrease of more than 30 percent in the authority to obligate funds, and the transit account's authority would decrease by about 65 percent, compared with CBO's baseline projections.
- *Revenues credited to the trust fund could be increased*— for example, by raising existing taxes on motor fuels or other transportation-related products and activities or by imposing new taxes on highway users, such as vehicle-miles traveled (VMT) taxes. The staff of the Joint Committee on Taxation (JCT) estimates that a one-cent increase in taxes on motor fuels— primarily gasoline and diesel fuel—would raise about $1.5 billion each year for the trust fund. If lawmakers chose to meet obligations projected for the trust fund solely by raising revenues, they would need to increase motor fuel taxes by an amount between 10 cents and 15 cents per gallon, starting in fiscal year 2015.
- *The trust fund could continue to receive supplements from the Treasury's general fund.* Lawmakers could maintain funding for surface transportation programs at the average amounts provided in recent years, but to do so they would need to transfer $18 billion in 2015 and between $13 billion and $18 billion every year thereafter through 2024. Spending resulting from such general fund transfers could be paid for by reducing other spending or by increasing broad-based taxes, or such transfers could add to deficits and thus increase federal borrowing.

The projected shortfalls in the Highway Trust Fund have generated interest in greater use of borrowing by state and local governments to finance highway projects. In particular, state and local governments (and some private entities) can use tax-preferred bonds that convey subsidies from the federal government in the form of tax exemptions, credits, or payments in lieu of credits to finance road construction. Similarly, some of those governments make use of direct loans from the federal government to finance projects.

Federal policies that encourage partnerships between the private sector and a state or local government may facilitate the provision of additional transportation infrastructure, but a review of those projects offers little evidence that public-private partnerships provide additional resources for roads except in cases in which states or localities have chosen to restrict spending through self-imposed legal constraints or budgetary limits.

Only a small number of highway projects in the United States have involved public-private partnerships with private financing. Some that have been financed through tolls have failed financially because the private-sector partners initially overestimated their revenues and as a result have been unable to fully repay their projects' debts. Perhaps as a response, projects that are still under construction rely less on tolls as a revenue source; more commonly, private partners are compensated from a state's general funds, thus limiting the private risk of not being repaid and leaving the risk of lower-than-expected revenues to the public partner.

Regardless of its source, however, borrowing is only a mechanism for making future tax revenues or user fee revenues available to pay for projects sooner; it is not a new source of revenues. Borrowing can augment the funds available for highway projects, but revenues that are committed for repaying borrowed funds will be unavailable to pay for new transportation projects or other government spending in the future.

SPENDING FOR HIGHWAYS AND MASS TRANSIT

Almost all spending on highway infrastructure and transit projects in the United States is funded publicly. Although the private sector participates in building, operating, and maintaining projects, the federal government and state and local governments typically determine which projects to undertake and how much to spend on them. Despite several prominent examples, private spending on highway projects constitutes only a small fraction of the total.

Almost three-quarters of all public spending on highways is by state and local governments: In 2013, state and local governments spent $110 billion, and the federal government spent $46 billion. Almost all federal highway spending is capital spending, which is used to build and improve highways; by contrast, about 40 percent of the total for state and local governments is capital spending and 60 percent is for operations and maintenance. Real (inflation-adjusted) total spending on highways by federal, state, and local governments increased in the 1980s and 1990s, but it has fallen off since then. Public-private partnerships that involve private financing have accounted for about one-half of one percent of all spending on highways during the past 25 years. Spending on transit programs is much less than for highways but has generally grown—especially spending by state and local governments—during recent decades (see Figure 1).[1]

THE HIGHWAY TRUST FUND

The federal government's surface transportation programs are financed mostly through the Highway Trust Fund, an accounting mechanism in the federal budget that comprises two separate accounts, one for highways and one for mass transit. The trust fund records specific cash inflows from revenues collected through excise taxes on the sale of motor fuels, trucks and trailers, and truck tires; taxes on the use of certain kinds of vehicles; and interest credited to the fund. The Highway Trust Fund also records cash outflows for spending on designated highway and mass transit programs, mostly in the form of grants to states and local governments.

Spending from the Highway Trust Fund is controlled by two types of legislation:

- Authorization acts that provide budget authority (which allows the government to incur financial obligations that will result in immediate or future outlays of federal funds), mostly in the form of contract authority (which permits the government to enter into contracts or to incur obligations in advance of appropriations), and
- Annual appropriation acts, which customarily set limits on the amount of contract authority that can be obligated in a given year.

The Moving Ahead for Progress in the 21st Century Act of 2012 (MAP-21) is the most recent law authorizing highway and transit programs; its authorizations expire on September 30, 2014, at the end of the current fiscal year. MAP-21 provided a total of about $51 billion in contract authority for highway and transit programs in 2014; the 2014 obligation limitations total about $50 billion.

Excise taxes on motor fuels account for 87 percent of the Highway Trust Fund's revenue, mostly from the tax of 18.4 cents per gallon on gasoline and ethanol-blended fuels.[2] Receipts from the gasoline tax now constitute almost two-thirds of the fund's total revenues (see Table 1). Under current law, all but 4.3 cents per gallon of that tax is set to expire on September 30, 2016. If that occurs, its remaining receipts will no longer be credited to the trust fund but instead will go into the Treasury's general fund. The second-largest share, accounting for about one-quarter of the fund's revenues, comes from the diesel fuel tax of 24.4 cents per gallon. The remainder comes from other taxes and from a very small amount of interest that is credited to the fund. Most of the revenue from motor fuel taxes is credited to the highway account of the trust fund, but 2.86 cents per gallon goes into the mass transit account, which receives about 13 percent of the trust fund's total revenues and interest.

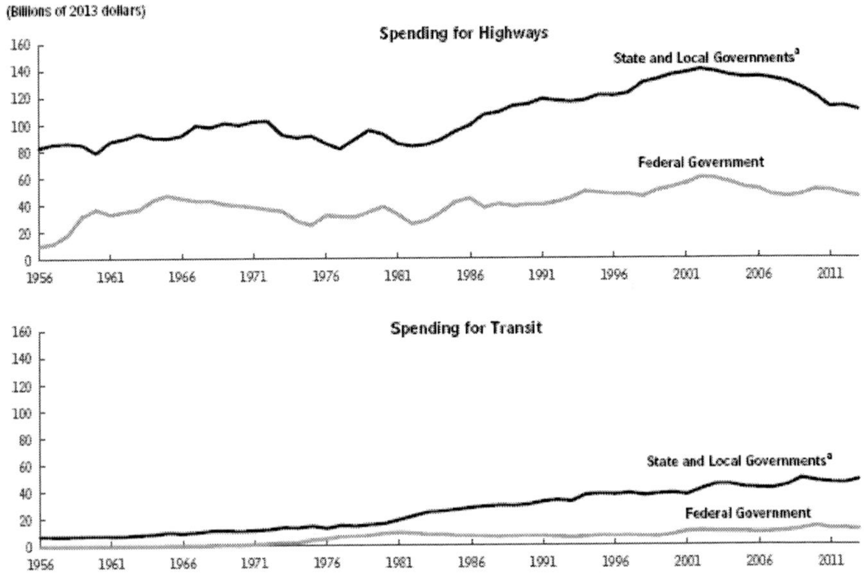

Figure 1. Spending for Highways and Transit, by Level of Government.

Table 1. Estimated Revenues Credited to the Highway Trust Fund, by Source, 2014 (Billions of dollars)

	Highway Account	Transit Account	Total	Share of Total Trust Fund Revenues and Interest[a] (Percent)
Gasoline Tax	20.1	3.7	23.8	63
Diesel Tax	8.1	1.1	9.1	24
Tax on Trucks and Trailers	3.5	0	3.5	9
Use Tax on Certain Vehicles	1.0	0	1.0	3
Tire Tax on Trucks	0.4	0	0.4	1
	____	____	____	____
Total	33.2	4.8	38.0	100

Source: Congressional Budget Office.

[b] In 2014, CBO estimates, a small amount of interest will be credited to the Highway Trust Fund, in keeping with provisions of the Hiring Incentives to Restore Employment Act of 2010.

History of the Trust Fund's Balances

For several decades, the balances in the highway account were relatively stable or growing, but since 2001, receipts have consistently fallen below expenditures.[3] (The transit account was not established until 1983 and, until 2006, it had a different accounting treatment that makes historical comparisons inapplicable.) During the 1980s and the first half of the 1990s, balances in the highway account held steady in the vicinity of $10 billion. The most recent increase in the gasoline tax occurred in 1993, and after the Taxpayer Relief Act of 1997 redirected 4.3 cents of that tax from the general fund to the Highway Trust Fund, the unexpended balance in the highway account began to grow rapidly, reaching almost $23 billion in 2000. In 1998, the Transportation Equity Act for the 21st Century (known as TEA-21) authorized spending that was sufficient to gradually draw down those balances. As a result of that legislation and the Safe, Accountable, Flexible, Efficient Transportation Equity Act: A Legacy for Users (SAFETEA-LU), which was enacted in 2005, outlays have generally exceeded revenues since 2001.

Since 2006, when certain accounting changes specified in TEA-21 took effect, spending from the transit account has grown and, since 2008, has exceeded revenues credited to the account. TEA-21 and SAFETEA-LU authorized spending from the account that has exceeded revenues credited to the fund by between $3 billion and $4 billion every year.

Because of looming shortfalls, since 2008 lawmakers have enacted legislation to transfer a total of more than $54 billion to the trust fund—mostly from the Treasury's general fund. Those intragovernmental transfers have allowed the fund to maintain a positive balance, but they did not change the amount of receipts collected by the government. Despite those transfers, at the end of fiscal year 2013, the trust fund's balances totaled only $6 billion.

Projections of Outlays and Revenues in 2014

According to CBO's estimates, the highway account will end fiscal year 2014 with a balance of $2 billion—at the end of 2013, that balance was $4 billion (see Table 2). By CBO's estimates, outlays from the highway account will total $45 billion in 2014, but revenues and interest earnings will amount to just $33 billion for the year. To bridge most of the gap, MAP-21 transferred $10 billion of general funds to the highway account in 2014 (following a $6 billion transfer in 2013).

Table 2. Projections of the Highway Trust Fund's Accounts Under CBO's April 2014 Baseline

(Billions of dollars, by fiscal year)	2013	2014	2015	2016	2017	2018	2019	2020	2021	2022	2023	2024
					Highway Account							
Start-of-Year Balance	10	4	2	a	a	a	a	a	a	a	a	a
Revenues and Interest[b]	32	33	34	34	34	34	34	34	34	34	34	34
Intragovernmental Transfers[c]	6	10	0	0	0	0	0	0	0	0	0	0
Outlays[d]	43	45	45	45	45	46	46	46	47	48	48	49
End-of-Year Balance	4	2	a	a	a	a	a	a	a	a	a	a
						Transit Account						
Start-of-Year Balance	5	2	1	a	a	a	a	a	a	a	a	a
Revenues and Interest[b]	5	5	5	5	5	5	5	5	5	5	5	5
Intragovernmental Transfers[c]	0	2	0	0	0	0	0	0	0	0	0	0
Outlays[d]	7	8	8	8	8	9	9	9	10	10	10	10
End-of-Year Balance	2	1	a	a	a	a	a	a	a	a	a	a
Memorandum:												
Cumulative Shortfall[a]												
Highway account	n.a.	n.a.	-10	-21	-32	-43	-55	-67	-79	-92	-106	-120
Transit account	n.a.	n.a.	-2	-6	-9	-13	-18	-22	-27	-32	-38	-44

Source: Congressional Budget Office. Note: n.a. = not applicable.

[a] Beginning in fiscal year 2015, CBO projects, revenues credited to the highway and transit accounts of the Highway Trust Fund will be insufficient to meet the fund's obligations. Under current law, the trust fund cannot incur negative balances nor is it permitted to borrow to cover unmet obligations presented to the fund. Under the Deficit Control Act of 1985, however, CBO's baseline for highway spending must incorporate the assumption that obligations incurred by the Highway Trust Fund will be paid in full. The cumulative shortfalls shown here thus are estimated on the basis of spending that is consistent with obligation limitations contained in

CBO's April 2014 baseline—adjusted for projected inflation—for highway and transit spending. To meet obligations as they come due, the Department of Transportation estimates, the highway account must maintain cash balances of at least $4 billion, and the transit account must maintain balances of at least $1 billion. As a result, under CBO's baseline projections, the highway account will probably have to delay some of its payments during the summer of 2014.

[b] Some taxes that are credited to the Highway Trust Fund are scheduled to expire on September 30, 2016—among them the taxes on certain heavy vehicles and tires and all but 4.3 cents of the federal tax on motor fuels. Under the rules that govern CBO's baseline projections, however, these estimates reflect the assumption that all of those expiring taxes would be extended.

[c] The Moving Ahead for Progress in the 21st Century Act required certain intragovernmental transfers, mostly from the U.S. Treasury's general fund, to the Highway Trust Fund. Those amounts totaled about $18 billion. CBO's baseline does not reflect an assumption that additional transfers from the general fund would occur.

[d] Outlays include amounts that are transferred between the highway and transit accounts. CBO estimates that those amounts will total about $1 billion annually.

The situation is similar for the transit account, which will end fiscal year 2014 with a balance of $1 billion, CBO estimates, down from $2 billion a year earlier. Revenues and interest earnings are projected to amount to $5 billion in 2014, but outlays are expected to total more than $8 billion. MAP-21 transferred $2 billion of general funds to the transit account in 2014.

Unless additional funds are provided (either through an increase in revenues or through additional transfers to the general fund), the disparity between the receipts credited to the fund and outlays from the fund will require DOT to delay its reimbursements to states for the costs of construction. CBO estimates that such a delay would probably take effect sometime during the summer of 2014 for projects funded from the highway account and sometime in the first half of 2015 for transit projects. Such a slowdown in payments occurred in 2008 when DOT announced that balances in the highway account had fallen below what it needed to reimburse states for the bills presented to the fund. Because deposits into the fund are made only twice each month, DOT has testified that it would need to delay payments if cash balances fell below $4 billion in the highway account or below $1 billion in the transit account.[4]

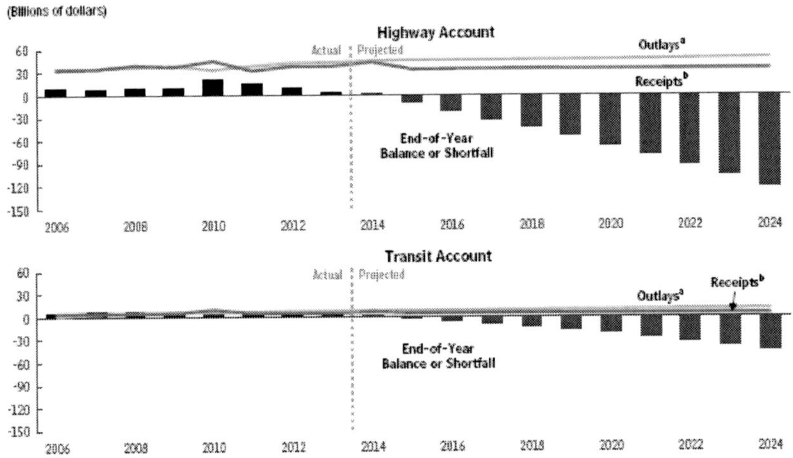

Source: Congressional Budget Office.

Notes: Under current law, the Highway Trust Fund cannot incur negative balances nor is it permitted to borrow to cover unmet obligations presented to the fund. Under the Deficit Control Act of 1985, however, CBO's baseline for highway spending must incorporate the assumption that obligations incurred by the Highway Trust Fund will be paid in full.

[a] Projections of outlays are calculated by adjusting the obligation limitations set for the current year to account for projected inflation.

[b] Projections of receipts are based on market conditions, and they incorporate an assumption under CBO's April 2014 baseline that some taxes (including taxes on certain heavy vehicles and tires and all but 4.3 cents of the federal tax on motor fuels) that are credited to the Highway Trust Fund but scheduled to expire on September 30, 2016, would be extended. The receipts line includes revenues credited to the Highway Trust Fund and intragovernmental transfers, mostly from the U.S. Treasury's general fund. Since 2008, those transfers (including amounts transferred in fiscal year 2014) have totaled about $54 billion.

Figure 2. Receipts, Outlays, and Balance or Shortfall for the Highway Trust Fund Under CBO's April 2014 Baseline.

Projections of Outlays and Revenues from 2015 through 2024

CBO's baseline projections reflect the assumptions that expiring excise taxes would be extended and that obligations from the trust fund would grow at the rate of inflation. Under those assumptions, CBO projects, shortfalls in both accounts of the trust fund would grow steadily larger over the next decade because revenues from the excise taxes are expected to grow very little, but spending would continue to rise (see Figure 2).5 By 2024, the cumulative shortfalls would total about $120 billion for the highway account and about $44 billion for the transit account, CBO estimates.

Revenues generated by excise taxes and credited to the Highway Trust Fund are projected to rise from about $38 billion in 2014 to about $39 billion in 2024, mostly because annual increases in revenues from taxes on the use of diesel fuel and on truck sales are expected to be largely offset by annual declines in revenues from the tax on gasoline. Tax revenues from diesel fuel and truck sales are projected to increase, on average, by about 3 percent annually over the 2014–2024 period. In contrast, revenues from the tax on gasoline are projected to decline at an average annual rate of 1 percent over that period, mainly because of mandated increases in corporate average fuel economy standards.[6]

If lawmakers do not address the projected shortfalls, all revenues credited to the Highway Trust Fund in 2015 will be used to meet obligations made before that year. (Most obligations involve capital projects that take years to complete. The Federal-Aid Highway program, for example, typically spends about 25 percent of its budgetary resources in the year funds are first made available for spending; the rest is spent over the next several years.) Most of the trust fund's current obligations will therefore be met using tax revenues that have not yet been collected. At the end of 2013, for example, $66 billion in contract authority for highway programs had been obligated but not yet spent and another $28 billion was available to states but not yet obligated. As a result, if states were given no further authority to spend, another three years' worth of motor fuel taxes would need to be collected just to meet the highway account's obligations at the end of 2013 plus any new obligations from contract authority made available before 2014. Tax receipts dedicated to the highway account are projected to be about $34 billion per year over the next three years. For the transit account, collections of almost five years' worth of taxes, at about $5 billion per year, would be needed to meet current obligations and any new obligations from contract authority made available before 2014.[7]

Options for Addressing Projected Shortfalls in the Highway Trust Fund

Lawmakers have three primary options for addressing the projected shortfalls in the Highway Trust Fund:

- Reduce spending on highways and transit,
- Increase taxes dedicated to the trust fund, or
- Transfer general revenues to supplement the trust fund.

Of course, many combinations of such changes are possible.

Reduce Spending from the Trust Fund

Policymakers might want to address projected shortfalls by limiting federal spending for highways and mass transit to the amount of revenue generated by users. That reduction in spending would probably have significant negative consequences for the condition and performance of the nation's highway and mass transit infrastructure. In addition, unless some other federal spending was increased or federal taxes lowered, the reduction in federal spending would slow economic growth and employment during the next few years relative to what it would otherwise be. Over the longer term, the smaller amount of infrastructure would impose a drag on economic performance, but the smaller amount of federal debt stemming from the lower level of spending would provide an economic boost.

If lawmakers chose to avert projected shortfalls solely by cutting spending, then the trust fund would be unable to support any new obligations in 2015, probably significantly delaying investment in infrastructure and halting numerous transportation projects across the country. Neither the highway account nor the transit account would be able to support new obligations in 2015 because reimbursements to states for multiyear projects already under way would be expected to exceed the estimated revenue collections for that year. The highway account would be able to support new obligations in 2016, but the transit account would not (see Figure 3). Such sudden shifts in the amount of annual spending authority would probably make program administration and planning difficult for DOT as well as for state and local grant recipients.

Over the 2015–2024 period, the highway account would see a decrease in obligational authority of more than 30 percent, relative to CBO's baseline, and such authority for the transit account would decrease by about 65 percent. For example, such a cut would reduce obligations for highway programs from current projections of about $45 billion per year, on average, to about $32 billion per year, on average, from 2015 through 2024.

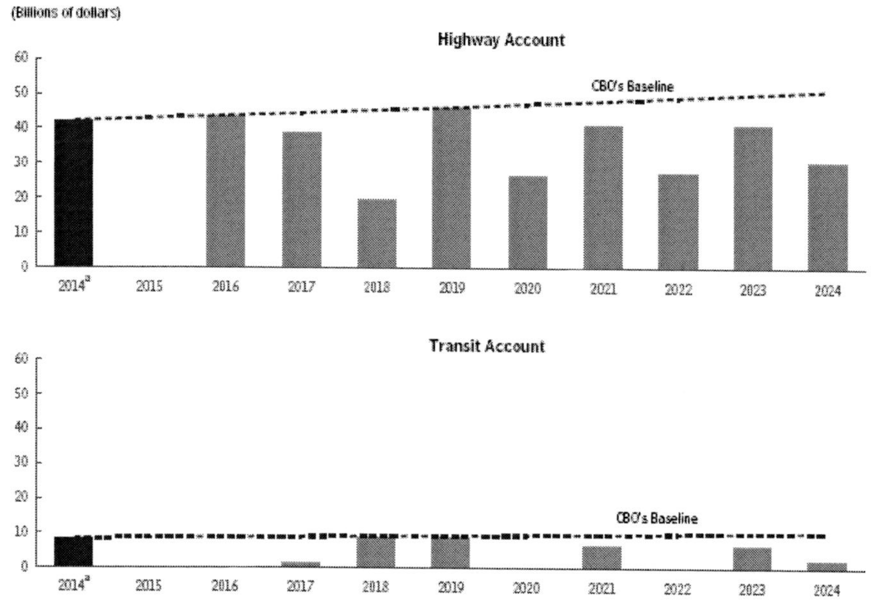

Source: Congressional Budget Office.

Note: The figure shows the new commitments that could be provided from the highway and transit accounts of the Highway Trust Fund as long as the minimum balance in the highway account was at least $4 billion and the minimum balance in the transit account was at least $1 billion and the obligation limitation for each account did not exceed the amounts projected in CBO's April 2014 baseline.

[a] Data for 2014 represent the obligation limitations contained in the Consolidated Appropriations Act, 2014, and contract authority that is exempt from those limitations.

Figure 3. Estimated New Commitments That Could Be Accommodated by the Highway Trust Fund With No Changes in Receipts.

Similarly, such a cut would reduce obligations for transit projects from current projections of about $10 billion per year, on average, to about $4 billion per year, on average, for the 2015–2024 period.

The consequences of such reductions in federal spending could be ameliorated, at least in part, if state and local governments responded to the reduction in federal funds by increasing their own spending through some combination of raising additional revenues, shifting spending from other purposes, and borrowing.

If total funding for investment in highways and mass transit was significantly reduced, then it would be especially important to allocate the remaining funding, and to use that infrastructure, in the most effective way.

Specifically, the negative consequences of a substantial reduction in funding could be partly alleviated if the remaining spending was focused on projects with especially large benefits and if people's use of highways and mass transit was focused on the highest-value uses (for example, through taxes on vehicle-miles traveled or congestion pricing).[8] In addition, the economic efficiency of each dollar of funding could be improved if the federal government limited its support to projects (such as the Interstate highways) that offer significant benefits to more than one state, leaving state and local governments to fund projects with more localized benefits. If the people who benefit from a project bear its costs, the likelihood is diminished that too large a project (or too many projects) will be undertaken or that too many infrastructure services will be consumed relative to the resources needed to provide them.

Increase Taxes Dedicated to the Trust Fund

Another approach to bringing the trust fund's finances into balance would be to increase its revenue—for example, by raising the taxes on motor fuels or by imposing mileage-based, or VMT, taxes.[9] Increasing the charges that highway users pay also could promote more efficient use of the system. Economic efficiency is enhanced when highway users are charged according to the marginal (or incremental) costs of their use, including the external costs that their highway use imposes on society. A combination of a fuel tax and a VMT tax that accounts for the type and weight of a vehicle and the location and time of its use could provide incentives for reducing driving's social costs and could generate funds for federal spending on highways. But generating additional funds that way would raise questions of fairness, including, for example, whether the structure of user charges would impose relatively greater burdens on low-income and rural users.

Fuel Taxes. Excise taxes credited to the Highway Trust Fund come primarily from taxes on gasoline, ethanol-blended fuels, and diesel fuels. Those excise taxes were last increased in 1993, and their purchasing power is about 40 percent below that in 1993. If those taxes had been adjusted to keep pace with the consumer price index, for example, the tax on gasoline, which is currently 18.4 cents per gallon, would be about 30 cents per gallon, and the tax on diesel fuel, currently 24.4 cents per gallon, would be about 40 cents per gallon.

According to JCT's estimates, a one-cent increase in the taxes on motor fuels, effective October 1, 2014, would raise about $1.5 billion annually for the Highway Trust Fund over the next 10 years.[10] If lawmakers chose to meet obligations projected for the trust fund solely by raising revenues, they would have to increase the taxes on motor fuels by between 10 cents and 15 cents per gallon, starting in fiscal year 2015. (That increase would return fuel taxes to roughly the level they were in 1993, after adjusting for the effects of inflation.)

Fuel taxes offer a mix of positive and negative characteristics in terms of many people's conception of equity. They satisfy a "user pays" criterion—that those who receive the benefits of a good or service should pay its cost. But they also can impose a larger burden relative to income on people who live in low-income or rural households because those people tend to spend a larger share of their income on transportation. Fuel taxes impose a burden even on households that do not own passenger vehicles by raising transportation costs, which are reflected in the prices of purchased goods.

Fuel taxes have two desirable characteristics that are related to economic efficiency: They cost relatively little to implement (the government collects taxes from fuel distributors, and users pay the taxes when they purchase fuel), and they offer users some incentive to curtail fuel use, thus reducing some of the social costs of travel. However, a fuel tax discourages some travel too much and other travel too little, because it does not reflect the large differences in cost for use of crowded roads compared with uncrowded roads or for travel by trucks that have similar fuel efficiency but cause different amounts of pavement damage. Moreover, for a given tax rate on fuels, the incentive to reduce mileage-related costs diminishes over time as more driving is done in vehicles that are more fuel efficient.

VMT Taxes. VMT taxes provide stronger incentives for efficient use of highways than fuel taxes do because VMT taxes are better aligned with the costs imposed by users. Most of those costs—including pavement damage, congestion, accidents, and noise—are tied more closely to the number of miles vehicles travel than they are to fuel consumption.

For VMT taxes to significantly improve efficiency, however, they would need to vary greatly according to vehicle type, time of travel, place of travel, or some combination of such characteristics. For example, because pavement damage increases sharply with vehicle weight but decreases with the number of axles on a vehicle, the portion of VMT taxes assessed to maintain pavement could be small or nonexistent for passenger vehicles but substantial for heavy-duty trucks, particularly those with high weight per axle. Similarly, VMT taxes could be higher for any travel on crowded urban roads during peak hours than for travel in off-peak hours or on roads that are less congested.

In fact, a system of VMT taxes would not need to apply to all vehicles on every road. There already exist less comprehensive systems of direct charges for road use: Toll roads, lanes, and bridges are common in the United States, and several states and foreign countries place weight-and-distance taxes on trucks. Expansion of existing systems could focus on highly congested roads or on entry points into congested areas, and such targeted approaches would cost less to implement if they required relatively simple equipment to be placed in vehicles. Alternatively, the focus could be on specific vehicle types: Although trucks (excluding light-duty trucks), for example, constitute only 4 percent of all vehicles in the United States, they account for roughly 25 percent of all costs that highway users impose on others, including almost all of the costs associated with pavement damage.

The costs of implementing VMT taxes include capital costs for equipment and operating costs for metering, payment collection, and enforcement. The cost to establish and operate a nationwide program of VMT taxes is uncertain and difficult to estimate because projections so far are based mainly on small trials that have used a variety of evolving technologies and because the cost would depend on whether VMT taxes would vary by time, place, or type of vehicle. Although the costs of charging drivers are declining with improvements in technology, the costs remain higher than those for collecting revenues through the motor fuel taxes. The idea of imposing variable VMT taxes also has raised concerns about privacy: The collection process could give the government access to specific information about when and where individual vehicles are used.

Transfer Money from the General Fund

Lawmakers could choose to continue to supplement the Highway Trust Fund with general revenues, thus providing more money for highways and transit systems than is collected from excise taxes dedicated to those purposes. To continue funding for surface transportation programs at the average amounts provided in recent years, adjusted for inflation, lawmakers would need to transfer $18 billion to the Highway Trust Fund in 2015, CBO estimates. That transfer would cover a projected cumulative shortfall in the Highway Trust Fund of $13 billion and allow the trust fund to maintain cash balances of at least $4 billion in the highway account and at least $1 billion in the transit account. Subsequently, lawmakers would need to transfer $13 billion in 2016; such transfers would need to increase gradually to $18 billion by 2024 to maintain current spending, adjusted for inflation. At that pace, by 2024, CBO projects, general fund transfers would account for about one-third of the receipts credited to the Highway Trust Fund.

Spending that resulted from such transfers could be paid for by reducing other spending or by increasing broad-based taxes, such as income taxes; or it could add to deficits and thus increase federal borrowing. Reductions in other spending would mean that the benefits of the spending on transportation would be at least partially offset by a reduction in whatever benefits that other spending would have provided. Boosting the already-high federal debt would have long-term negative effects on the economy.

Increasing broad-based taxes would offer advantages and disadvantages compared with raising taxes on highway users. Two arguments can be made in support of using such a source of funding for highways. First, some benefits of better highway infrastructure are distributed more broadly than to just highway users. For example, reducing transportation costs for suppliers and customers increases efficiency by allowing businesses to specialize more in terms of the products and services they produce and the materials they use. Second, large amounts could be raised through small changes in tax rates. JCT has estimated that raising all tax rates on ordinary individual income by 1 percentage point would yield an average of $69 billion per year from 2014 to 2023—more than all of the current Highway Trust Fund taxes combined.[11] Moreover, funding highways through broad-based taxes does not impose a larger burden relative to income on rural or low-income users (unlike some taxes on fuel use).

In other respects, however, the use of general revenues poses disadvantages. In particular, the approach gives users no incentive to drive less or to use less fuel, and it does not satisfy the principle that a user-pays system may be fairest and most efficient. Moreover, even a small increase in existing tax rates would hamper economic efficiency by discouraging work and saving and by encouraging people to shift income from taxable to nontaxable forms and to shift spending from ordinary to tax-deductible goods and services.

FINANCING HIGHWAYS

The projected shortfalls in the Highway Trust Fund have generated interest in increasing the amount of spending that can be sustained in the near term by encouraging state and local governments to rely more heavily on debt financing. Most highway projects now are paid for with current state or federal revenues. Apart from increasing their own taxes or cutting other spending, state and local governments or other public entities could finance additional spending on highways in a number of ways, including one or more of the following:

- Issuing tax-preferred government bonds,
- Obtaining federal loans or loan guarantees, or
- Joining with a private partner to obtain private financing.

Tax-preferred government bonds include tax-exempt bonds (among them private activity bonds, or PABs) and tax credit bonds, both of which transfer some of the cost of borrowing from state and local governments and the private sector to the federal government in the form of forgone federal tax revenues. Investors are generally willing to accept a relatively low rate of return on tax-preferred bonds because interest income is exempt from federal (and many state) taxes and because those bonds are backed by the taxing authority of the public entity.

Federal loans or loan guarantees can reduce state and local governments' borrowing costs, depending on the terms of the loan, in part because the federal government assumes the risk that would be borne by a lender and paid for by a borrower in the form of higher interest rates. A current federal loan program offers state and local governments an opportunity to borrow money for highways and certain other transportation projects at interest rates that are based on the long-term Treasury rate.

Assessments of the experience with private financing of highways in the United States suggest that turning to a private partner does not typically yield additional financing, although doing so may speed the provision of financing and make new roads available sooner than they would have been otherwise. Private financing can provide the capital necessary to build a new road, but it comes with the expectation of repayment and a future return, the ultimate source of which is either tax revenues collected by a government or fees from road users, like tolls—the same sources that are available to governments. All told, the total cost of the capital for a highway project, whether that capital is obtained through a government or through a public-private partnership, tends to be similar once all relevant costs are taken into account. Regardless of its source, financing is only a mechanism for making future tax or user fee revenues available to pay for projects sooner; it is not a new source of revenues.

Tax-Preferred Bonds

The federal government provides several types of tax preferences to subsidize infrastructure financing. *Tax-exempt bonds* use the well-established tax preference of paying interest that is not subject to federal income tax. Such bonds can be issued to finance the functions of state and local governments or, in the case of PABs, certain types of projects undertaken by the private sector. A second, more recently developed type of tax preference for infrastructure financing is associated with *tax credit bonds*. Such bonds come in two basic forms: those that provide a tax credit to the bondholder in lieu of paying interest and those that allow the bond issuer to claim a tax credit. (For issuers with no tax liability, the credit in the second scenario takes the form of a payment from the Secretary of the Treasury. Such bonds are known as direct-pay tax credit bonds.) Tax-exempt and tax credit bonds alike transfer some of the cost of borrowing from state and local governments and the private sector to the federal government, either in the form of forgone federal tax revenues or, in the case of direct-pay tax credit bonds, a federal outlay.

Tax preferences provide federal support for infrastructure financing while generally allowing state and local governments to exercise broad discretion over the types of projects they finance and the amount of debt they issue. However, tax preferences are not governed by the annual appropriation process, so lawmakers exercise less oversight over their continuation and use than is applied to federal grant and loan programs. Also, because forgone revenues are not identifiable in the federal budget, the use of tax preferences can mask the full scope of the government's financial activities. Using some types of tax-preferred bonds can be an inefficient way to deliver a federal financial subsidy to state and local governments. With a tax exemption for interest income, for example, state and local borrowing costs (and the costs of the private entities that make use of PABs) are reduced by significantly less than the amount of forgone federal revenues; the remainder of that tax expenditure accrues to bond buyers in the highest income tax brackets. Subsidizing borrowing through the use of payments made directly to borrowers can be more efficient—in terms of the benefits to state and local governments per dollar of federal cost— and more conducive to budgetary review and control.[12]

Tax-Exempt Government Bonds

Federal tax exemptions for interest income from government bonds (and qualified PABs) allow issuers of such debt to sell bonds that pay lower rates of interest than do taxable bonds. Because purchasers of tax-exempt bonds demand a return that is at least as high as the after-tax yield they could obtain from comparable taxable bonds, the amount by which the return from tax-exempt bonds is lower than the yield on comparable taxable debt depends on the income tax rate of the marginal (or market-clearing) buyer of tax-exempt bonds. Thus, the amount of subsidy that state and local governments receive by issuing tax-exempt bonds is determined not by an explicit decision of the federal government, but indirectly by the federal tax code and the financial circumstances of potential investors.

JCT estimates that the tax exemption for state and local debt resulted in $32 billion of forgone federal revenues in 2012; for the subsequent five years, it estimates that tax-exempt debt will reduce revenues by an additional $191 billion. According to data from the Internal Revenue Service, tax-exempt bonds issued between 1991 and 2011 to finance highway and other transportation projects (both for new construction and to refund existing transportation debt) accounted for between about one-eighth and one-fifth of the total value of tax-exempt bonds issued that can be classified by the type of project financed. Thus, a rough estimate of the tax expenditure for transportation bonds in 2012 would be between $4 billion and $6 billion. Data from proprietary sources suggest that highway bonds may account for as much as one-half of all tax-exempt debt issued to finance transportation projects.[13]

Private Activity Bonds

Private activity bonds are tax-exempt bonds that typically are used to finance large infrastructure and other projects primarily undertaken by a private entity. Thus, PABs essentially provide financing to private businesses or individuals; a qualified governmental unit serves as a conduit between those entities and the purchaser of the bond. Only certain PABs are tax exempt. Bonds that meet the necessary criteria are known as qualified private activity bonds and may be issued to finance a wide range of infrastructure (and other) projects, including those for transportation.

SAFETEA-LU allowed tax-exempt PABs to be issued for certain surface transportation projects, but the law placed a cap of $15 billion on the issuance of such bonds. According to DOT (as of April 18, 2014), bonds with a value of $4.6 billion have been issued for 11 projects in all since 2005. DOT allocated another $5.2 billion of that $15 billion to projects that, although approved, have not started and could use PABs in the future; roughly 30 percent of that amount has been allocated during the past 12 months. That leaves slightly more than $5 billion available for future applicants. However, the almost $10 billion in bonds currently issued or allocated under the $15 billion cap may overstate the amount of PABs that those projects will use eventually, because some projects that received a PAB allocation have switched to other forms of financing. For example, in May 2013, DOT allocated about $4.4 billion from PABs to seven projects that had not yet issued bonds. By April 2014, however, only five of them had issued PABs, all for amounts that were significantly less than originally allocated.

Giving private entities access to the tax-exempt market using PABs lowers the cost of capital for those borrowers and can promote infrastructure projects when state and local governments have self-imposed limits on borrowing. But, like tax-exempt government bonds, PABs result in forgone tax revenues. And, to the extent that private funding was available without PABs, albeit at a higher cost, only projects of marginal value would be unable to receive financing without them.

Because of the growing number of projects seeking to use PABs, some financial market analysts are concerned that the limit on their use will be reached soon. Development of large, complex infrastructure projects often takes years, so financial analysts are seeking certainty that PABs will be available if they choose to apply for them. In his 2015 budget proposal, the President proposed raising the cap, by $4 billion, to $19 billion. According to JCT's estimates, such an additional allocation would begin to be used sometime in 2017.

Tax Credit Bonds

Starting in the late 1990s, the Congress turned to tax credit bonds as a way to finance public expenditures. In their early form, those bonds allowed their holders to receive a credit against federal income tax liability instead of—or in addition to—the cash interest typically paid on the bonds. The amount of the credit equals the credit rate, which is set by the Secretary of the Treasury, multiplied by the face amount of the bond.

Tax credit bonds offer some advantages over other types of tax-preferred bonds, such as tax-exempt bonds. Because bondholders pay taxes on the amount of credit they claim, tax credit bonds do not result in investors in high marginal tax brackets receiving a portion of the forgone tax revenues. Rather, the revenues forgone by the federal government through tax credit bonds reduce state and local borrowing costs dollar for dollar, a more efficient use of federal resources than that resulting from tax-exempt bonds. Tax credit bonds also allow the amount of federal subsidy to be determined explicitly, rather than depending on other federal polices (such as marginal income tax rates).

The American Recovery and Reinvestment Act of 2009 authorized Build America Bonds, tax credit bonds that were sold only in 2009 and 2010. State and local governments issued the bonds either as traditional tax credit bonds or, if certain conditions were met, as direct-pay tax credit bonds (known as qualified Build America Bonds). In contrast to earlier tax credit bonds, Build America Bonds have an interest rate (or coupon) that is set by the issuer rather than by the Secretary of the Treasury. For the direct-pay bonds, the federal government provided payments directly to issuing state and local governments equal to 35 percent of the interest, in lieu of a tax credit going to the bondholder. The amount of that financing subsidy is greater than the reduction in the interest costs that those state and local governments would have realized if they had issued traditional tax-credit bonds because, in the latter case, the bond buyer claiming the tax credit would have had to be compensated with additional interest income for the resulting tax liability.

The interest subsidies provided by direct-pay tax credit bonds appear as outlays in the federal budget, making the cost more transparent and, in principle, enabling comparison with other federal outlays for the same purposes. Also, because the yields provided to holders of direct-pay tax credit bonds are similar to the yields of other taxable securities, direct-pay tax credit bonds are more attractive to tax-exempt entities than other tax credit bonds are and may therefore increase the pool of funds available to state and local governments to finance infrastructure projects and other activities.

The President's budget proposal for 2015 includes a direct-pay tax credit bond with a credit equal to 28 percent of each interest payment. By allowing state and local governments to substitute taxable for tax-exempt bonds, the proposal would increase taxable interest income, boosting federal revenues by $59 billion between 2015 and 2024, according to JCT. Because the proposal also would increase subsidy payments to state and local governments (which are recorded in the federal budget as outlays) by an estimated $64 billion, the net effect would be to increase the cumulative 10-year deficit by $4 billion.[14]

FEDERAL LOANS AND LOAN GUARANTEES

The federal government also subsidizes borrowing by state and local governments by providing and guaranteeing loans for infrastructure. Such credit assistance can reduce state and local governments' costs because it can facilitate borrowing at interest rates that are lower than otherwise might be available, and it may open additional access to the capital markets. Specifically, in providing loans and loan guarantees, the federal government assumes the risk that would be borne by a lender and paid for by a borrower in the form of higher interest rates.

The Federal Credit Reform Act of 1990 (FCRA) established rules for calculating the budgetary costs of direct loans and explicit loan guarantees issued by the federal government. The budgetary cost of federal credit assistance programs is recorded as the net present value of the cash flows to and from the government—the loan amount and the expected repayments—when the loan is disbursed to recipients.[15] That subsidy cost represents an estimate of the net cost that the government bears. In contrast, the cash flows associated with that loan between the Treasury, an agency, and borrowers occur over time and are not recorded in the budget.

An important aspect of the budgetary treatment of federal credit programs is that agencies must receive an appropriation equal to the estimated subsidy cost before they can make or guarantee a loan.[16] In the case of direct loans, FCRA specifies that loan repayments are unavailable for future spending; those repayments are already accounted for in the estimated net present value of the loan, so they are not available to "revolve" into new loans. Such a revolving fund is the model on which many state infrastructure banks are based. However, for the federal government, those repayments represent part of the financing for the original loans and are implicit in the subsidy calculation. Allowing loan repayments to be used for new loans—without any additional appropriation to cover the subsidy costs of the new loans—would raise the effective FCRA subsidy cost of the original loans to 100 percent (the same as for grants).

FCRA accounting, however, does not provide a comprehensive measure of the economic cost of credit assistance. Through its use of Treasury rates for discounting, FCRA implicitly treats market risk—a type of risk that investors require compensation to bear—as having no cost to the government. Specifically, FCRA's procedures incorporate the expected cost of defaults on government loans or loan guarantees but not the cost of risk associated with uncertainty about the magnitude and timing of those defaults. Investors require compensation—a “market risk premium”—to bear that risk. That premium on a risky loan or guarantee compensates investors for the increased likelihood of sustaining a loss when the overall economy is weak and resources are scarce; that likelihood is reflected in higher expected returns and lower prices for assets that carry more market risk. Taxpayers bear the investment risk for federal credit obligations. By omitting the cost of market risk and thereby understating the economic cost of federal credit obligations, FCRA accounting may lead policymakers to favor credit assistance over other forms of aid that have a similar economic cost.[17]

Loans Made Under the Transportation Infrastructure Finance and Innovation Act

DOT administers a loan program under the Transportation Infrastructure Finance and Innovation Act of 1998 (TIFIA) that provides credit assistance to state and local governments to finance highway projects and other types of surface transportation infrastructure. The TIFIA program offers subordinated federal loans for up to 35 years at interest rates that are based on the rate for Treasury securities of similar maturity. (On May 1, 2014, the interest rate on the 30-year Treasury bond was 3.41 percent.) TIFIA assistance may be used for up to 49 percent of a project’s cost. Combined with other federal grants and credit assistance, TIFIA loans can be part of a package of federal assistance that funds up to 80 percent of the cost of a project.

MAP-21 made several changes to the TIFIA program, notably increasing the amount of budget authority for the subsidy cost of the program’s loans from $122 million per year in the previous authorization for highway and transit programs to $750 million in 2013 and $1 billion in 2014. As of April 28, 2014, about $720 million of that budget authority was uncommitted. Since 2012, TIFIA subsidy rates for direct loans have averaged about 9 percent. If that subsidy rate continued in effect, the $1.75 billion in subsidies authorized by MAP-21 would finance more than $19 billion in loans.

MAP-21 also authorized master credit agreements and created an extra interest rate subsidy for projects in rural areas. Master credit agreements would allow DOT to make commitments of future TIFIA loans, contingent on future authorizations, to a group of projects secured by a common revenue source. Under provisions of MAP-21, rural projects receive a minimum of 10 percent of the funds appropriated and are eligible to receive loans at half the Treasury rate. Such an interest rate subsidy makes a project relatively less expensive for the sponsors and relatively more expensive for the federal government. It may result in federal loans for projects that would not otherwise generate enough revenue to cover the costs of financing the projects.

Proposals for a Federal Infrastructure Bank

In recent years, the Congress has considered several proposals for establishing a federal bank to fund infrastructure projects through loans and grants.[18] In recent years, the President's budget has included a request to create a similar entity.[19]

Whether federal credit assistance is provided through an existing federal agency or a newly created special entity, however, it would involve similar budgetary costs to the federal government. The support offered for surface transportation by most proposed infrastructure banks would not differ substantially from the loans and loan guarantees already offered by DOT through its TIFIA program. Therefore, differences between the existing TIFIA program and an infrastructure bank would primarily be operational, concerning the types of infrastructure to fund, the kinds of credit assistance to provide, the selection process for projects, the amount of leverage to provide for federal funds, and the amount of private-sector participation to encourage or require. For example, an infrastructure bank could focus on financing transportation infrastructure, or it could define infrastructure more broadly to include sewers, wastewater treatment facilities, drinking water supply facilities, broadband Internet access, or even schools. In principle, an infrastructure bank could use any of several methods to finance projects, including federal loans, lines of credit, and guarantees for private loans.

CBO has previously analyzed an illustrative federal infrastructure bank—one that is representative of certain recent proposals but that would focus on surface transportation programs.[20] That entity, which would be federally funded and controlled, would select new, locally proposed construction projects for funding on the basis of several criteria, including the projects' costs and benefits, and it would provide financing for the projects through loans and loan guarantees. To repay the loans, projects would have to use tolls, taxes, or other dedicated revenue streams. Financial assistance could be provided to any consortium of partners with an eligible project, such as a group of state and local entities or a group of nongovernmental partners. The bank could provide the subsidy amounts needed to compensate private-sector investors for benefits that accrue to the general public and to the economy at large.

Such an infrastructure bank could have a limited role in enhancing investment in surface transportation projects by providing new federal subsidies (in the form of loans or loan guarantees) to certain large projects, potentially including multijurisdictional or multimodal projects, and by allowing the benefits of potential projects to be more readily compared in a competitive selection process.

A key limitation of such a bank is that many surface transportation projects would not be good candidates for its support, because most projects do not involve toll collections or other mechanisms to collect funds directly from project users or other beneficiaries.

PRIVATE FINANCING

Only a small number of highway projects in the United States have involved public-private partnerships with private financing.[21] Assessments of those projects indicate that such partnerships may accelerate the availability of financing—for example, by circumventing states' self-imposed limits on borrowing—but they do not generally result in additional financing. Some of the projects that have been financed through tolls have failed financially because the private-sector partners initially overestimated their revenues and as a result have been unable to fully repay their projects' debts. Perhaps as a response, projects that are still under construction rely less on tolls as a revenue source; more commonly, private partners are compensated from a state's general funds, thus limiting the private risk of not being repaid and leaving the risk of lower-than-expected revenues to the public partner.

Increasingly, public-private partnerships also have replaced the funds obtained through private means (at market rates) with tax-exempt bonds or bonds that provide a credit against taxes owed. That change has brought the projects more in line with the way states typically finance infrastructure projects, lowering the private partners' costs at the expense of costs to federal taxpayers and increasing the amount of the government's implicit equity and risk. In doing so, newer projects may have diminished the incentives associated with private financing to control costs and to be completed quickly.

In addition, more recent agreements have reduced private partners' debt-service payments—that is, interest payments on any money borrowed to finance the projects— by increasing the share of financing provided by the state or locality or by the federal government. Accordingly, the financing provided by the TIFIA program or by tax-exempt private activity bonds has become increasingly prominent for highway projects that involve public and private partners.

The history of privately financed roads in the United States encompasses 29 projects that are either under way or have been completed during the past 25 years. The value of the contracts for those projects totals $24 billion, a little more than one-half of one percent of the approximately $4 trillion that all levels of government spent on highways over the period. (Both of those amounts are in 2013 dollars.) In the past few years, the number of partnerships for road projects with private financing has increased; two-thirds of the $24 billion in contracts has been committed in the past five years.

The amount of risk transferred to private partners has varied from project to project. In some instances, the financial risk was borne primarily by taxpayers, who were responsible for repaying debt incurred by the private partner. Under one program in Florida, for example, private businesses finance each project entirely with private debt that is to be repaid over a predetermined time—usually five years—with future grants from the federal government, state funds, and revenues from tolls collected from users of the completed road. The state's guarantee of repayments eliminates much of the transfer of risk that takes place with other privately financed projects. Thus, the financing is essentially public, and the structure of the public-private partnership is similar to that of an approach without private financing. In other instances, the private partner has borne more of the risk of the investment—specifically, some of the private partners' money might be lost if the project did not produce revenues as expected.

Over the past 25 years, 10 privately financed projects— of various sizes but all involving contracts of at least $50 million—have been completed (see Table 3). A review of those projects offers little evidence that public-private partnerships provide additional resources for roads except in cases in which states or localities have chosen to restrict spending through self-imposed legal constraints or budgetary limits. To varying degrees, the projects that made use of private financing were in states in which the government could have issued bonds to finance the work through traditional means. In some cases, however, the use of a public-private partnership accelerated a project's access to financing by circumventing restrictions that states have imposed on themselves and that limit their ability to issue additional debt. (Earlier financing of a road project adds value when it allows the public to enjoy the benefits of the new road sooner than would otherwise be possible.)

Several such projects are still under construction (see Table 4). New public-private partnerships have sought to reduce their borrowing costs by relying on publicly subsidized borrowing through the TIFIA program and through PABs issued by local municipalities; the PABs have tax advantages that lower the private partner's debt-service payments. All but one of those projects have made use of federal subsidies through the TIFIA program. That choice of financing constitutes a return to some features of the traditional approach in which the public sector—the federal government, in particular—retains greater risks, especially the risk of default. For instance, the South Bay Expressway, which had received some financing from the TIFIA program, illustrates what can happen to taxpayers as the ultimate equity holders. The project filed for Chapter 11 bankruptcy in March 2010, finally emerging in May 2011. The new financing and ownership structure required by the bankruptcy court imposed a loss of 42 percent on federal taxpayers, replacing the original TIFIA investment with a package of debt and equity worth only 58 percent of the original investment.[22] New public-private parternerships also typically secure state or local loans or grants as part of their financing. In the other cases, project managers who are responsible for a project's financing have had to take out bank loans. That source of private capital was more attractive during the recent economic downturn as interest rates fell relative to the yields for bonds in municipal bond markets (including those of PABs).

BUDGETARY PRINCIPLES FOR THE TREATMENT OF PROJECTS WITH COMPLEX FINANCING

Under the principles that govern federal budgeting, the budgetary treatment of complex financing arrangements—those that involve an intermediary other than the Treasury raising money in private capital markets on behalf of the federal government—should depend on its economic substance: who controls the program and its budget, who selects the managers, who provides the capital, and who owns the resulting entity.[23] Is the activity governmental (that is, initiated, controlled, or funded largely by the government for governmental purposes) or is it an initiative of the private sector (driven by market forces independent of the government)?

An investment that is essentially governmental should be shown in the budget whether it is financed directly by the Treasury or indirectly by a third party that is borrowing on behalf of the government. Activities need not be conducted by a federal agency to be classified as governmental and included in the budget. When doubt exists about whether a program should be recorded in the federal budget, those same principles indicate that "borderline agencies and transactions should be included in the budget unless there are exceptionally persuasive reasons for exclusion."[24]

Table 4. Highway Projects Under Way That Use Public-Private Partnerships With Private Financing

	I-595 Manage dLanes	North Tarrant Express Segment s 1 &	Port of Miami 2Tunnel	I-635 LBJ Freeway	I-95 HOV/H OT Lanes	Mid-town Tun-nels	Presi-dio Park-way	Ohio River Bridges East End Cross-ing	North Tarrant Express Sege-ment 3A
				Description of the Project					
Start of Construction	2009	2010	2010	2011	2012	2012	2013	2013	2014
Expected Completion	2014	2015	2014	2016	2015	2017	2015	2016	2018
Location	Fla.	Tex.	Fla.	Tex.	Va.	Va.	Calif.	Ind.	Tex.
Revenue Source	Tolls/ Taxes	Tolls	Taxes	Tolls	Tolls	Tolls	Taxes	Tolls/ Taxes	Tolls
Road Length (Miles)	11	13	1	13	29	1	2	8	6
			Sources of Financing (Millions of 2013 dollars)						
Private									
Debt	829	0	362	0	0	0	167	0	0
Equity	231	452	85	713	280	272	46	78	413
Public									
TIFIA program	640	690	362	902	300	422	150	0	524
Private activity bonds[a]	0	422	0	643	253	675	0	677	271
Other[b]	246	609	329	520	90	719	0	395	169
Total Cost	*1,946*	*2,173*	*1,138*	*2,779*	*923*	*2,089*	*365*	*1,150*	*1,377*

Source: Congressional Budget Office based on data from the Federal Highway Administration.

Note: HOV = high-occupancy vehicle; HOT = high occupancy/toll; TIFIA = Transportation Infrastructure Finance and Innovation Act.

[a] Private activity bonds are issued by or on behalf of a state or local government to finance a private project.

[b] federal formula grants.

Likewise, spending financed by all forms of agencies' borrowing, including debt not backed by the full faith and credit of the U.S. government, appears in the budget. However, bond proceeds or repayable equity investments are not recorded as federal receipts; they are a means of financing a project—not the ultimate source of capital, which is the income that will be generated by their operation.

End Notes

[1] For more information on infrastructure spending, see Congressional Budget Office, Public Spending on Transportation and Water Infrastructure (November 2010), www.cbo.gov/publication/21902.

[2] The total gas tax is 18.4 cents per gallon. Of that, 18.3 cents is credited to the Highway Trust Fund, and 0.1 cent goes to the Leaking Underground Storage Tank Trust Fund. (The Omnibus Budget Reconciliation Act of 1993 increased the gas tax by 4.3 cents, from 14.1 cents to 18.4 cents; the added receipts were not initially credited to the trust fund but instead went into the Treasury's general fund.)

[3] In 2010, the trust fund saw a significant decrease in outlays because states spent funds from the general fund of the Treasury that were appropriated in the American Recovery and Reinvestment Act of 2009. That act did not require states to match federal funds or even to contribute funds to projects, and the same projects that were eligible for funding from the Highway Trust Fund were eligible for funding under the act.

[4] Department of Transportation, Office of Inspector General, Refinements to DOT's Management of the Highway Trust Fund's Solvency Could Improve the Understanding and Accuracy of Shortfall Projections, CR-2012-071 (March 2012), p. 22, www.oig.dot. gov/node/5736.

[5] CBO constructs its baseline in accordance with provisions set forth in the Balanced Budget and Emergency Deficit Control Act of 1985 and in the Congressional Budget and Impoundment Control Act of 1974.

[6] For more information, see Congressional Budget Office, How Would Proposed Fuel Economy Standards Affect the Highway Trust Fund? (May 2012), www.cbo.gov/publication/43198.

[7] See Office of Management and Budget, Budget of the U.S. Government, Fiscal Year 2015: Appendix (April 2014), www.whitehouse.gov/omb/budget/Appendix. At the end of fiscal year 2013, the balance in the transit account was about $2 billion, but unspent contract authority for transit programs totaled $14 billion in obligated balances and $9 billion in unobligated amounts.

[8] For a comprehensive discussion of the benefits and challenges of congestion pricing, including options for its design and implementation for highways, see Congressional Budget Office, Using Pricing to Reduce Traffic Congestion (March 2009), www.cbo.gov/publication/20241.

[9] See Congressional Budget Office, Alternative Approaches to Funding Highways (March 2011), www.cbo.gov/publication/22059.

[10] Because excise taxes reduce the tax base of income and payroll taxes, higher excise taxes would lead to a reduction in revenues from income taxes and payroll taxes. The estimates shown here do not reflect those reductions. Those reductions would amount to about 25 percent of the estimated increase in excise tax receipts.

[11] See Congressional Budget Office, Options for Reducing the Deficit: 2014 to 2023 (November 2013), p. 106, www.cbo.gov/budget-options/ 2013/44687.

[12] For more information, see Congressional Budget Office and Joint Committee on Taxation, Subsidizing Infrastructure Investment with Tax-Preferred Bonds (October 2009), www.cbo.gov/publication/41359.

[13] See Joint Committee on Taxation, Estimates of Federal Tax Expenditures for Fiscal Years 2012–2017, JCS-1-13 (February 2013), p. 40, http://tinyurl.com/kasohdx; Internal Revenue Service, Statistics of Income, “Table 2. Long-Term Tax-Exempt Governmental Bonds, by Bond Purpose and Type of Issue,” http://tinyurl.com/pvw7znq; and Thomson Reuters, “Transportation Highlights,” The Bond Buyer Yearbook (various issues).

[14] See Congressional Budget Office, An Analysis of the President’s 2015 Budget (April 2014), www.cbo.gov/publication/45230.

[15] The net present value is the single number that expresses a flow of current and future income (or payments) in terms of an equivalent lump sum received (or paid) today.

[16] In contrast, no appropriations are necessary for the periodic revisions to subsidy estimates that agencies make to reflect actual experience with loans and guarantees. Permanent indefinite budget authority exists for those revisions, which are recorded in the budget as increases or decreases in outlays.

[17] Moreover, subsidy rates computed under FCRA exclude federal administrative costs, even those that are essential for preserving the value of the government’s claim to future repayments, such as loan-servicing and collection costs; those costs are accounted for separately in the budget. For more information, see Congressional Budget Office, Fair-Value Accounting for Federal Credit Programs (March 2012), www.cbo.gov/publication/ 43027.

[18] Other government programs that provide credit assistance for infrastructure projects include the Environmental Protection Agency’s grants for states’ revolving loan funds for water projects and states’ infrastructure banks, all capitalized with federal funds and administered by states.

[19] Other Congressional proposals to establish an infrastructure bank include providing bond insurance to issuers.

[20] See Congressional Budget Office, Infrastructure Banks and Surface Transportation (July 2012). www.cbo.gov/publication/43361.

[21] For additional information on the experience with public-private partnerships, see the testimony of Joseph Kile, Assistant Director for Microeconomic Studies, Congressional Budget Office, before the Panel on Public-Private Partnerships, House Committee on Transportation and Infrastructure, Public-Private Partnerships for Highway Projects (March 5, 2014), www.cbo.gov/publication/45157.

[22] Randall Jensen, “Tollway Exits Chapter 11: TIFIA Ends Up Taking a Haircut,” Bond Buyer (May 6, 2011), http://tinyurl.com/3fn8nvj.

[23] See Congressional Budget Office, Third-Party Financing of Federal Projects (June 2005), www.cbo.gov/publication/16554.

[24] The President’s Commission on Budget Concepts, Report of the President’s Commission on Budget Concepts (October 1967).

In: The Highway Trust Fund
Editor: Jonathan Caulfield
ISBN: 978-1-63482-012-7
© 2015 Nova Science Publishers, Inc.

Chapter 2

PROJECTIONS OF HIGHWAY TRUST FUND ACCOUNTS UNDER CBO'S AUGUST 2014 BASELINE*

Congressional Budget Office

Projections of Highway Trust Fund Accounts Under CBO's August 2014 Baseline (Billions of dollars, by fiscal year)

	2013	*2014*	*2015*	*2016*	*2017*	*2018*	*2019*	*2020*	*2021*	*2022*	*2023*	*2024*
Highway Account												
Start-of-Year Balance	10	4	11	[a]	[a]	[a]	[a]	[a]	[a]	[a]	[a]	[a]
Revenues and Interest[b]	32	33	33	34	34	34	34	34	34	34	34	34
Intragovernmental Transfers[c]	6	18	0	0	0	0	0	0	0	0	0	0
Outlays[dd]	43	45	45	45	45	46	46	46	47	48	48	49
End- of- Year Balance	4	11	[a]	[a]	[a]	[a]	[a]	[a]	[a]	[a]	[a]	[a]
Transit Account												
Start-of-Year Balance	5	2	3	[a]	[a]	[a]	[a]	[a]	[a]	[a]	[a]	[a]
Revenues and Interest[b]	5	5	5	5	5	5	5	5	5	5	5	4

* This is an edited, reformatted and augmented version of a document issued by the CBO, August 27, 2014.

	2013	*2014*	*2015*	*2016*	*2017*	*2018*	*2019*	*2020*	*2021*	*2022*	*2023*	*2024*
Intragovernmental Transfers[c]	0	4	0	0	0	0	0	0	0	0	0	0
Outlays[d]	7	8	8	8	8	9	9	9	10	10	10	10
End- of- Year Balance	2	3	a	a	a	a	a	a	a	a	a	a
Memorandum												
Cumulative Shortfall[a]												
Highway Account	n.a.	n.a.	-2	-13	-25	-36	-48	-60	-73	-86	-100	-115
Transit Account	n.a.	n.a.	*	-4	-7	-11	-16	-20	-25	-31	-36	-42

Notes: Details may not add to totals because of rounding. n.a. = not applicable.

* = shortfall of less than $500 million.

[a] Beginning in fiscal year 2015, CBO projects, revenues credited to the highway and transit accounts of the Highway Trust Fund will be insufficient to meet the fund's obligations. Under current law, the trust fund cannot incur negative balances, nor is it permitted to borrow to cover unmet obligations presented to the fund. Under the Balanced Budget and Emergency Deficit Control Act of 1985, however, CBO's baseline for highway and transit spending must incorporate the assumption that obligations incurred by the Highway Trust Fund will be paid in full. As a result, the cumulative shortfalls shown here are estimated on the basis of spending that would occur if obligations from the fund each year were equal to the obligation limitations enacted for 2014, adjusted for projected inflation. To meet obligations as they come due, the Department of Transprotation estimates, the highway account must maintain a cash balance of at least $4 billion and the transit account must maintain a balance of at least $1 billion.

[b] Some of the taxes that are credited to the Highway Trust Fund are scheduled to expire on September 30, 2016, among them the taxes on certain heavy vehicles and tires and all but 4.3 cents of the federal tax on motor fuels. However, under the rules governing baseline projections, these estimates reflect the assumption that all of the expiring taxes credited to the fund continue to be collected.

[c] Sections 40201 and 40251 of the Moving Ahead for Progress in the 21st Century Act (Public Law 112-140) and section 2002 of the Highway and Transportation Funding Act of 2014 (Public Law 113-159) required certain intragovernmental transfers, mostly from the general fund of the Treasury, to the Highway Trust Fund. CBO's baseline does not reflect an assumption that additional transfers from the general fund would occur.

[d] Outlays include amounts transferred between the highway and transit accounts. CBO estimates that those amounts would total about $1 billion annually.

In: The Highway Trust Fund
Editor: Jonathan Caulfield

ISBN: 978-1-63482-012-7
© 2015 Nova Science Publishers, Inc.

Chapter 3

HIGHWAY TRUST FUND: DOT HAS OPPORTUNITIES TO IMPROVE TRACKING AND REPORTING OF HIGHWAY SPENDING*

United States Government Accountability Office

WHY GAO DID THIS STUDY

In recent years, dedicated revenues to the Highway Trust Fund have been eroding, resulting in fewer resources to fund surface transportation projects and requiring, between 2008 and 2014, transfers of over $50 billion in general revenues.

Four operating administrations within DOT—FHWA, FTA, NHTSA, and FMCSA—receive funding from the Highway Trust Fund for programs administered by these agencies, and FHWA receives the largest share (81 percent of the agency's authorizations in fiscal year 2013).

GAO was asked to review how Highway Trust Fund monies are being used to help ensure that sound choices and investment decisions about future funding are made. This report examines what is known about the types of projects, activities, and federal administrative functions and expenses supported by DOT using Highway Trust Fund monies in fiscal year 2013.

* This is an edited, reformatted and augmented version of a United States Government Accountability Office publication, No. GAO-15-33, dated October 2014.

To address this request, GAO obtained and analyzed fiscal year 2013 federal obligation data from DOT's operating administrations, reviewed relevant documentation, and interviewed FHWA, FTA, FMCSA, NHTSA, and DOT officials.

WHAT GAO RECOMMENDS

GAO recommends that the Secretary of Transportation direct the FHWA Administrator to explore the costs, feasibility, and options for collecting and publicly reporting consistent aggregate project-level spending data. DOT agreed with our recommendation. DOT also provided technical comments, which we incorporated, as appropriate.

WHAT GAO FOUND

In fiscal year 2013, operating administrations within the Department of Transportation (DOT) collected and reported some information on the types of activities and administrative expenses funded from the Highway Trust Fund, but did so with varying levels of detail. The Federal Highway Administration (FHWA) obligated about $41 billion in fiscal year 2013, most of which ($39 billion) was apportioned to states through the federal-aid highway program. FHWA tracks federal-aid highway program obligations in its Fiscal Management Information System (FMIS), for individual project segments or contracts. This process allows FHWA to collect and report information on the types of activities (such as obligations for the construction of new roads or bridges) funded with Highway Trust Fund monies.

However, FHWA does not collect and report aggregate project-level data for the majority of projects on a routine basis. Aggregate project-level data would allow FHWA to track and report the total overall obligations of an entire project. While FHWA tracks and reports aggregate obligations for its "major projects" (projects with a total cost of $500 million or more), it does not collect and report aggregate obligations for other projects, which represented nearly 88 percent of all fiscal year 2013 spending. FHWA could collect and report aggregate obligations for all projects in FMIS, and FMIS has two existing data fields that could be used to collect this information. But according to FHWA officials, doing so would result in increased costs to

FHWA and states. FHWA officials attributed increased costs to, among other things, programming costs to make changes to FMIS to track these data; however, FHWA has not completed a cost analysis to estimate what the associated costs would be. FHWA is currently in the process of modernizing its FMIS database system. Exploring the costs, feasibility, and options for collecting and reporting consistent aggregate project-level obligations could aid FHWA in its oversight efforts, including its ability to more easily draw consistent data for its compliance reviews and to report information to Congress and the public about how the majority of federal funds from the Highway Trust Fund are being used.

The Federal Transit Administration (FTA), the National Highway Traffic Safety Administration (NHTSA), and the Federal Motor Carriers Safety Administration (FMCSA) also collect some information on activities funded with Highway Trust Fund monies. For example, FTA collects data on activities, such as obligations for bus and rail purchases, funded with Highway Trust Fund monies each year, and NHTSA and FMCSA collect and report data by grant program. In addition, within DOT, the FHWA, FMCSA, and NHTSA used Highway Trust Fund monies for a range of administrative expenses, such as personnel salaries and benefits and rent. FTA does not receive Highway Trust Fund monies for administrative expenses.

ABBREVIATIONS

DOT	Department of Transportation
FHWA	Federal Highway Administration
FMCSA	Federal Motor Carrier Safety Administration
FMIS	Fiscal Management Information System
FTA	Federal Transit Administration
FTE	full-time equivalent
MAP-21	Moving Ahead for Progress in the 21st Century Act
MCSAP	Motor Carrier Safety Assistance Program
NHTSA	National Highway Traffic Safety Administration
OST	Office of the Secretary of Transportation
TEAM	Transportation Electronic Award and Management

October 9, 2014

The Honorable David Vitter
Ranking Member
Committee on Environment and Public Works
United States Senate

Dear Senator Vitter:

The nation's surface transportation systems are critical to the economy and the movement of people and freight. Federal surface transportation programs are primarily funded by taxes on motor fuels and other truck-related taxes that are deposited into the Highway Trust Fund. In recent years, dedicated revenues from fuel taxes to the Highway Trust Fund have been eroding. Federal motor-fuel tax rates have not increased since 1993, and the 18.4 cents per-gallon tax on gasoline enacted in 1993 is worth about 11.5 cents today. This trend is expected to continue as demand for gasoline decreases with the introduction and adoption of more fuel-efficient and alternative fuel vehicles in the years ahead. In August 2014, the Congressional Budget Office estimated that to maintain current spending levels plus inflation between 2014 and 2024, the Highway Trust Fund will require about $157 billion more than it is expected to take in over that period. To maintain current spending levels and cover revenue shortfalls, between 2008 and 2014, Congress has transferred over $50 billion in general revenues to the Highway Trust Fund. And in August 2014, an extension of federal-aid highway programs through May 31, 2015, was enacted and will provide $10.8 billion in funding to the Highway Trust Fund, of which $9.8 billion will be transferred from the General Fund of the U.S. Treasury.[1] This approach may not be sustainable over the long term given competing demands for federal funding and the federal government's growing fiscal challenges. Congress and the Administration need to agree on a long-term, sustainable plan to fund surface transportation, and for this and other reasons, funding surface transportation is on GAO's High Risk List.[2]

The Moving Ahead for Progress in the 21st Century Act (MAP-21)[3] authorized Highway Trust Fund monies for programs administered by four operating administrations within the Department of Transportation (DOT)—the Federal Highway Administration (FHWA), the Federal Transit Administration (FTA), the National Highway Traffic Safety Administration (NHTSA), and the Federal Motor Carrier Safety Administration (FMCSA). Most of this funding is administered by FHWA, which distributes most of the funds to the states through formulas established in law under the federal-aid highway program. FHWA tracks federal-aid highway program obligations and the types of funded activities in its Fiscal Management and Information System (FMIS).[4] Non-state funding is tracked through the Delphi system. Highway Trust Fund monies are also used for other purposes, including for administrative expenses of the DOT's operating administrations. Currently, FHWA, NHTSA, and FMCSA receive monies from the Highway Trust Fund for administrative expenses, while FTA does not receive funding from the Highway Trust Fund for such expenses.

While Highway Trust Fund dollars are used for a wide range of activities, such as road or bridge improvements, information about these activities is not readily available to Congress and the public. For example, DOT's annual fiscal-year budget reports provide information on total spending at the program level, but do not provide detailed information about the types of activities and administrative expenses funded with Highway Trust Fund monies. Given the financial condition of the Highway Trust Fund, you asked us to provide information about how this funding is being used to help ensure that sound choices and investment decisions about future funding are made. We examined what is known about the types of projects, activities, and federal administrative functions and expenses supported by DOT using Highway Trust Fund monies in fiscal year 2013.

To address our reporting objective, we obtained and analyzed data on fiscal year 2013 obligations from the Highway Trust Fund for programs and administrative expenses administered by FHWA, FTA, FMCSA, and NHTSA— the DOT agencies that can directly obligate funds from the Highway Trust Fund. Specifically, we examined national level data on programs and activities that these agencies reported that could be readily aggregated from the obligation data. While each agency collects additional information about its programs and activities at the state and grantee level as part of its oversight and monitoring responsibilities, we focused only on what national level information could be aggregated from data on Highway Trust Fund obligations for fiscal year 2013. For FHWA, we obtained and analyzed data on federal-aid highway program obligations from FHWA's FMIS database. For FTA, we obtained and analyzed data on program obligations by program and by categories of activities from FTA's Transportation Electronic Award and Management (TEAM) system. Finally, for NHTSA and FMCSA, we analyzed data on obligations from Delphi, which is DOT's accounting system, for all grants funded from the Highway Trust Fund, to report total cumulative obligations in fiscal year 2013. We interviewed agency officials from each operating administration, reviewed agency documentation, and performed other steps to ensure the reliability of each operating administration's data, and we determined that the data were sufficiently reliable for the purposes of this report. In addition, we reviewed documents from and conducted interviews with each operating administration and the Office of the Secretary of Transportation (OST) to obtain additional information about Highway Trust Fund obligations for programs and administrative expenses. For FHWA, we reviewed agency documents and interviewed FHWA officials to gather additional information about its process for tracking project-level data in FMIS. We also reviewed relevant statutes, regulations, legislation, and other literature including prior GAO reports related to Highway Trust Fund obligations.

We conducted this performance audit from March 2014 to October 2014 in accordance with generally accepted government auditing standards. Those standards require that we plan and perform the audit to obtain sufficient, appropriate evidence to provide a reasonable basis for our findings and conclusions based on our audit objectives. We believe that the evidence obtained provides a reasonable basis for our findings and conclusions based on our audit objectives. A more detailed description of our scope and methodology is contained in appendix I.

BACKGROUND

Congress established the Highway Trust Fund in 1956 to hold highway user taxes that fund various surface transportation programs. The primary revenue sources for the Highway Trust Fund are federal excise taxes on motor fuels (gasoline, diesel, and special fuels taxes) and truck-related taxes (truck and trailer sales, truck tire, and heavy-vehicle use taxes). Fuel taxes provide about 89 percent of the excise tax income to the Highway Trust fund.[5] The Highway Trust Fund is divided into two separate accounts—Highway and Mass Transit Accounts. The Highway Account receives the majority (approximately 89 percent in fiscal year 2013) of the tax receipts allocated to the Highway Trust fund, including the majority of the fuel taxes.[6] All truck-related taxes are also deposited into the Highway Account.

The Highway Trust Fund primarily supports surface transportation programs administered by four DOT operating administrations—FHWA, FTA, FMCSA, and NHTSA. The Highway Account funds programs administered by FHWA, FMCSA, and NHTSA, and the Mass Transit Account funds FTA programs. For fiscal year 2013, MAP-21 authorized approximately $51 billion from the Highway Trust Fund to four DOT operating administrations, most of which was authorized to FHWA[7] (see fig. 1).

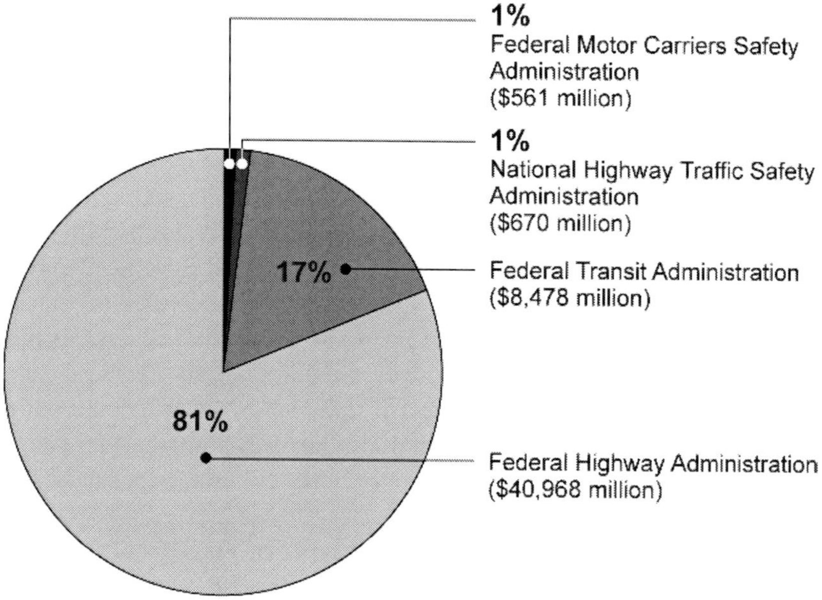

Source: GAO analysis of the Moving Ahead for Progress in the 21st Century Act, 2012. | GAO-15-33.

Note: FTA and NHTSA funding was authorized from both the Highway Trust Fund and the General Fund of the U.S. Treasury. In fiscal year 2013, FTA was authorized $10.6 billion, of which approximately $8.5 billion was from the Mass Transit Account of the Highway Trust Fund, and about $2.1 billion from the General Fund. NHTSA was authorized $803 million, of which $670 million was authorized from the Highway Trust Fund, and $133 million came from the General Fund.

Figure 1. Authorized Amounts from Highway Trust Fund by DOT Operating Administration, Fiscal Year 2013.

These agencies provide much of this funding directly to states, metropolitan-planning organizations, and transit agencies through formula and discretionary grants, and recipients select projects to be funded, subject to federal eligibility requirements.

- FHWA is primarily funded from the Highway Trust Fund.[8] Ninety percent of FHWA's authorized funds are for the federal-aid highway program. FHWA oversees this program and distributes much of this funding to states through annual apportionments established by statutory formulas. Apportioned funds are available for states to obligate for construction, reconstruction, and improvement of highways and bridges on eligible federal-aid highway routes, as well as for other purposes authorized in law.[9] While FHWA oversees and distributes funds to States, the responsibility for selecting specific highway projects generally rests with state DOTs and local-planning organizations, which have discretion in determining how to allocate available federal funds among various projects. Specifically, FHWA relies on its division offices—52 division offices located in each state, the District of Columbia, and Puerto Rico—to oversee projects funded through the federal-aid highway program and ensure these projects comply with federal requirements. However, FHWA is accountable for ensuring that the federal-aid highway program is delivered effectively, efficiently, and in compliance with established federal law.

  The remainder of FHWA's Highway Trust Fund funding (about 10 percent) is authorized for other programs including the Federal Lands Highway Program, which provides financial and engineering assistance for a network of public roads that serve the transportation needs of Federal and Indian Lands and FHWA's research and education activities. FHWA allocates Highway Trust funds to 28 agencies, such as the Department of Interior. See appendix II for additional information about FHWA's federal-aid highway and other spending.
- FTA receives funding from both the Mass Transit Account of the Highway Trust Fund for its Formula and Bus Grants and from the General Fund for its discretionary grants, which include the Capital Investment Grants programs. FTA distributes this funding to grant recipients for several activities, including financial and technical assistance to local and state public agencies to purchase, build, maintain, and operate transportation systems, and to support planning and operations for public transit systems, including bus, subway, and light rail. FTA works in partnership with states and other grant recipients to administer federal transit programs, provide financial assistance, policy direction, technical expertise, and some oversight.

State and local governments are ultimately responsible for executing most federal transit programs by matching and distributing federal funds and by planning, selecting, and supervising infrastructure projects and safety programs in accordance with federal requirements.

- NHTSA receives funding from both the Highway Trust Fund and the General Fund. It administers and distributes Highway Trust Fund monies by formula to states through various federal highway-safety grants, such as the State and Community Highway Safety Grant Program, which is a formula grant. This funding supports programs that work to reduce accidents from speeding, encourage the proper use of seat belts and child seats, reduce accidents from driving while intoxicated, prevent and reduce accidents between motor vehicles and motorcycles, and improve law enforcement services in motor-vehicle accident prevention and traffic supervision, among other things. NHTSA also coordinates through federal-state partnerships, regulates and issues safety standards for passenger vehicles, and addresses compliance issues with safety standards by performing tests, inspections, and investigations.
- FMCSA receives funding for programs from the Highway Trust Fund. FMCSA is charged with establishing and enforcing standards for motor carrier vehicles and operations, hazardous materials, and the movement of household goods, among other things. FMCSA also conducts compliance reviews of motor carriers' operations at their places of business as well as roadside inspections of drivers and vehicles, and can assess a variety of penalties, including fines and orders for noncompliant motor carriers to cease interstate operations. The largest of the federal motor carrier safety-grant programs funded from the Highway Trust Fund—the Motor Carrier Safety Assistance Program Grants—provides funding to states to reduce crashes, fatalities, and injuries related to commercial motor vehicle transportation.

MAP-21 also authorized Highway Trust Fund funds to be used for agency's administrative expenses. Currently, FHWA, FMCSA, and NHTSA all receive funding from the Highway Trust Fund for administrative expenses. FTA does not currently receive funding from the Highway Trust Fund for administrative expenses but requested such funding for fiscal year 2015.

HIGHWAY TRUST FUND SUPPORTED A RANGE OF ACTIVITIES, SUCH AS ROAD AND BRIDGE IMPROVEMENTS, AND EXPENSES, BUT COLLECTED AND REPORTED DATA VARY

FHWA collects and reports information on activities funded with obligations from the Highway Trust Fund. FHWA tracks this data for individual projects segments or contracts, but does not collect and report aggregate spending data at the project level for the majority of projects on a routine basis. FTA also collects data on the activities that are funded with Highway Trust Fund obligations each year, while NHTSA and FMCSA collect and report data on obligations from the Highway Trust Fund by grant programs. FHWA, NHTSA, and FMCSA also receive funding from the Highway Trust Fund for administrative expenses. Information on administrative obligations is available in annual budget requests.

FHWA Collects Some Information on Funded Highway Activities but Does Not Collect Some Project Data

In fiscal year 2013, FHWA obligated about $41 billion from the Highway Trust Fund, most of which (about $39 billion) was apportioned to states for activities to improve the nation's roadway and bridge infrastructure through the federal-aid highway program.[10] Our analysis of fiscal year 2013 federal-aid highway program obligations shows that states obligated most of this funding for road and bridge improvements (47 percent for roads in addition to 17 percent for bridges) (see fig. 2 below).[11] States obligated about 20 percent of Highway Trust Fund monies for project development activities including planning, engineering, and acquiring rights-of-way. Additionally, 9 percent was obligated for safety, enhancements and other improvements, including about 1 percent for sidewalks and bicycle trails.

We further analyzed road and bridge improvements and found that about 90 percent of obligations went toward reconstruction, resurfacing, and rehabilitation activities, while about 10 percent went toward new construction. Additional information about road and bridge improvements and funding by program are available in appendix II.

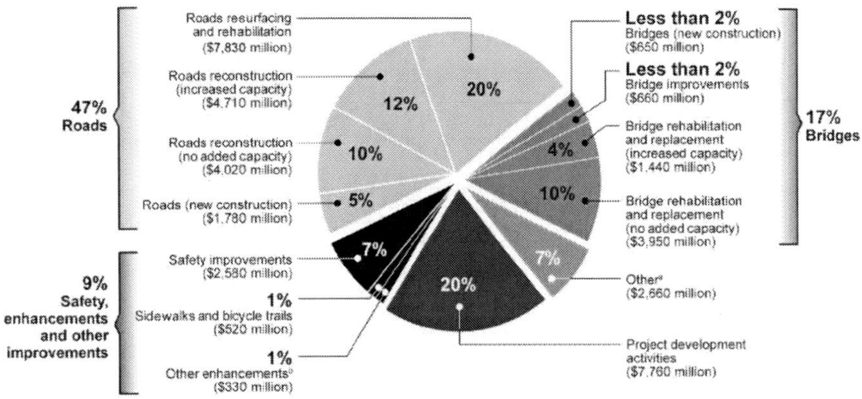

Source: GAO analysis of Federal Highway Administration data. | GAO-15-33.

Notes: Percentages do not total 100 percent due to rounding. In addition, this figure includes Highway Trust Fund obligations for Emergency Relief projects which totaled $132 million in fiscal year 2013.

[a]The other" category includes among other things, the Vehicle Weight Enforcement Program, tunnel activities, and ferryboats, and entries that did not have an improvement type classification. The total amount of obligations for entries that did not have an improvement type classification was about $4 million in fiscal year 2013.

[b]The "other enhancements" category includes cultural enrichment activities such as scenic beautification efforts and historic preservation.

Figure 2. Federal Highway Administration Highway Trust Fund Obligations by Improvement Type, Fiscal Year 2013.

While FHWA collects information in FMIS on the type of activities funded with Highway Trust Fund monies, it does not currently collect and report aggregate spending data at the project level for the majority of projects on a routine basis.[12] This is because FHWA tracks data in FMIS for individual project segments or contracts, but not for an entire project. For example, as shown in figure 3, a new highway project generally has four stages: (1) planning, (2) preliminary design and environmental review, (3) final design and right-of-way acquisition and (4) construction. Each stage can include multiple project segments or contracts over many years with distinct obligations at any given time, and FHWA does not currently link all project segments or contracts associated with an entire project in FMIS. Although FHWA is able to collect and report federal obligations by individual contract, it is not able to aggregate this information to collect and report total federal obligations for an entire project.

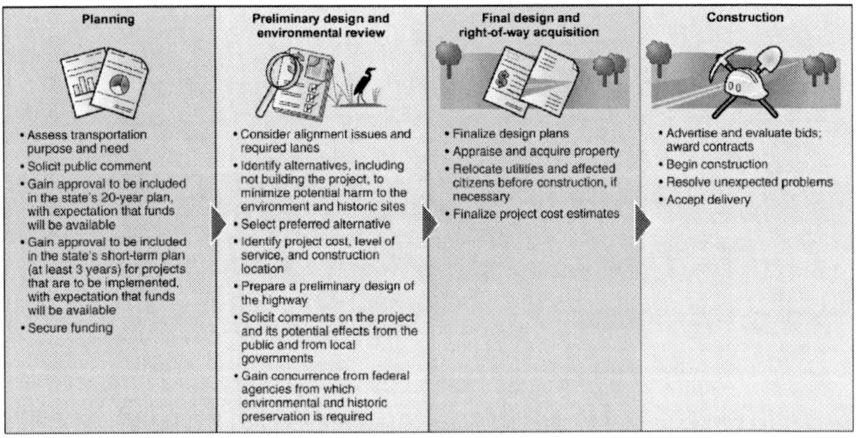

Source: GAO analysis of FHWA data. | GAO-15-33.

Figure 3. Key Stages and Typical Steps in a New Highway Project.

According to FHWA officials, FHWA is able to track and report aggregate spending data for "major projects," which are projects with a total cost of $500,000,000 or more, or other projects identified as such by the Secretary.[13] However, major projects are only a subset of all projects receiving federal-aid highway program funds, representing about 12 percent of all fiscal year 2013 federal-aid highway program spending (about $4.6 billion) for activities associated with 62 major projects.[14] See appendix III for additional information about federal obligations for major projects. FHWA could collect and report aggregate project-level data for all other projects in FMIS, but FHWA does not currently do so on a consistent basis. According to FHWA officials, currently, FMIS has two project-level data fields—"related project" and "state project numbers"— that could allow FHWA to identify project segments or contracts that are related to an entire project and track and identify total federal obligations. However, FHWA does not currently require state or division offices to use these data fields to link all project segments or contracts associated with an entire project. FHWA officials stated that although they have not conducted a cost analysis, they believe that requiring state and division offices to complete these two data fields in a consistent manner would result in increased costs to FHWA and states and would require additional resources. Specifically, FHWA would incur programming costs to make changes to FMIS to track this data. States could also incur costs to upgrade their own state systems to meet the new data-collection requirements. In addition, FHWA officials stated that not all states would be ready to adopt this change at the same time, leading to possible project delays and the potential for data reliability concerns. FHWA is preparing to modernize FMIS in fiscal year 2015, but according to officials, it does not have plans to make any changes to FMIS or to its policies that would require division offices to track aggregate project-level obligations in FMIS.

According to FHWA officials, it does not require states to track this information in FMIS because FHWA does not have a need to track all contracts associated with an entire project. According to FHWA officials, to obtain project data, FHWA will request such information directly from the state or division offices if it needs it. While FMIS is not a project management system, FHWA does use FMIS data for some purposes, which would be facilitated if FMIS did capture project level data. For example, FHWA uses FMIS data for its Compliance Assessment Program, a part of FHWA's Risk-Based Project Stewardship and Oversight process. Specifically, FHWA draws a project population sample for each division office from FMIS and then randomly selects projects to review. The purpose of these reviews is to help provide reasonable assurance that federal-aid highway projects comply with key federal requirements. However, because FMIS does not aggregate project-level information, FHWA must use an alternative method to draw its project sample, which involves selecting construction contracts that were authorized in the last 12 months.

In addition, others and we have previously found that developing the capability to track and measure costs over the life of a project could help FHWA to better target its oversight efforts, identify the extent of and reasons for problems, and identify and transfer lessons learned. In 2005, we reviewed FHWA's use of FMIS data to track and analyze trends in cost growth on projects. We found that FHWA had established performance goals and measures to contain costs on projects other than major projects, but was not yet using these goals to identify problems on a state-by-state or project-by-project basis in order to target its oversight activities.[15] We further found that FHWA could use project data in FMIS to measure the extent to which it was meeting its cost-related goal for non-major projects across states and that FHWA could use this information to identify trends and share this information with its division offices to transfer lessons learned. However, we found that because FMIS did not track project-level data, tracking cost growth on entire projects could be difficult. Best practices for conducting effective oversight of large infrastructure projects such as those in the federal-aid highway program overseen by FHWA include identifying lessons learned from the successes and setbacks that occur on projects and transferring those lessons to other projects to prevent mistakes from being repeated and promote improved oversight. We recommended that FHWA take actions to develop the capability to track and measure costs over the life of projects. FHWA neither concurred nor disagreed with this recommendation. FHWA has since taken steps to track aggregate costs for major projects in FMIS, but does not track aggregate costs for all other projects, which accounted for 88 percent of all projects receiving federal-aid highway obligations in fiscal year 2013. The capability to track and measure costs over the life of projects is important in order to be able to identify problems, target resources, and transfer lessons learned. Because one project can include many contracts over many years and FMIS does not automatically link contracts to projects, FHWA has little easily accessible information to help it determine the total overall costs of each project, other than the major projects. While FHWA officials told us that that tracking this information would be costly to FHWA and the states, it has not yet completed a cost analysis to estimate what these costs would be.

Similarly, in its 2005 review, the DOT Office of Inspector General found that as a result of not being able to aggregate related fields in FMIS, FHWA could not analyze overall project cost overruns and schedule delays.[16] The DOT OIG reported that unless FHWA develops an automated capability to identify the total cost of projects and any cost overruns, it would not have the most basic data needed to satisfy its grants management oversight responsibilities.

FTA, NHTSA, and FMCSA Collect Varying Levels of Data on Activities Funded with Highway Trust Fund Monies

FTA

FTA collects and reports information on activities funded with obligations from the Highway Trust Fund. FTA, through its grant management system—the Transportation Electronic Award and Management system, reports information on federal obligations in its annual statistical summaries, and makes this information publicly available on its website. The statistical summaries provide information about federal funds obligated each fiscal year for each of FTA's grant programs by categories of activities, such as obligations for "bus purchases" or "fixed guideway modernization" (such as rail purchases).

FTA obligated approximately $9 billion in fiscal year 2013 from the Mass Transit Account of the Highway Trust Fund through its Formula and Bus

Grants programs. These grant programs provided funding for a range of activities, such as to modernize existing rail systems, to increase access to transportation in rural areas, and to restore, replace and acquire buses and other equipment.[17] As shown in table 1, FTA obligated about $3 billion for activities to modernize or improve existing fixed guideway systems, which include among other things, purchases and rehabilitation of rail equipment, and station enhancements. FTA also obligated about $1.5 billion and $2 billion, respectively, for bus purchases and other bus activities in fiscal year 2013.

Table 1. Federal Transit Administration Obligations from the Highway Trust Fund, Fiscal Year 2013

Activity category	Total obligations (dollars in millions)	Percentage
Fixed Guideway Modernization[a]	$3,100	34 %
Rail Vehicles	400	4
Bus Other[b]	2,219	24
Bus Purchase	1,496	17
Operating Assistance	847	9
Bus Support	576	6
Planning[c]	247	3
Formula funding awarded to New Starts[d]	128	1
Other research and Activities[e]	81	1
Highway Trust Fund Total	$9,094	

Source: GAO Analysis of FTA data. | GAO-15-33

Note: Percentages do not total 100% due to rounding.

[a]Includes rail purchases and rehabilitation, station enhancements, support equipment and facilities, and other activities.

[b]Includes activities related to bus lines and facilities, power distribution, communication equipment, administrative and capital management, and other transit enhancements.

[c]Includes statewide, metropolitan, and consolidated planning activities.

[d]This funding was obligated from the Highway Trust Fund for programs, such as the Urbanized Area Formula program and the Fixed Guideway Modernization program and these funds were subsequently awarded to New Starts projects. The New Starts program funds new or expanded transit projects, primarily bus and rail.

[e]Includes the Rural Transit Assistance Program, research and university research, oversight reviews, safety and security, and management training activities.

FMCSA

FMCSA collects and reports obligations from the Highway Trust Fund at the grant program level, in its grant management data system, Grant Solutions, and Delphi, DOT's accounting system. As shown in table 2, FMCSA obligated about $298 million in fiscal year 2013, primarily through grants to states to improve commercial motor carrier vehicle safety, border enforcement, and vehicle license and information systems programs. The largest of FMCSA's grant programs, the Motor Carrier Safety Assistance Program (MCSAP), provided $213 million (about 71 percent of FMCSA's total federal obligations) to states to help develop or implement programs to reduce commercial motor vehicle-involved accidents, fatalities, and injuries, through safety activities such as inspections.[18] FMCSA also provided funding to states through its border enforcement ($32 million) and vehicle licensing and registration ($29 million) grant programs, as well as funding for investments in data programs such as the Performance and Registration Information System Management Grant Program ($5 million), among others. FMCSA collects other information about its grant programs as part of its oversight and monitoring responsibilities in other information systems. For example, FMCSA collects data on activities that were funded with MCSAP grants in its Analysis and Information Online Data Dashboard.

Table 2. Federal Motor Carrier Safety Administration Grant Programs' Obligations from the Highway Trust Fund, Fiscal Year 2013

Programs	Program description	Total obligations (dollars in millions)	Percentage
Motor Carrier Safety Assistance Program Grants[a]	Supports states in developing or implementing programs to improve commercial motor vehicle safety and reduce the number and severity of accidents.	$213	71 %
Border Enforcement Grants	Supports states in carrying out border commercial motor-vehicle safety programs and enforcement activities.	32	11

Programs	Program description	Total obligations (dollars in millions)	Percentage
Commercial Drivers License Program Improvement Grant	Supports states to reduce the number and severity of commercial motor vehicle crashes by ensuring that only qualified drivers receive commercial driver's licenses.	29	10
Commercial Vehicle Information Systems and Networks Deployment	Supports states to improve information technology exchanges between government agencies and the motor carrier industry.	16	5
Performance and Registration Information System Management Grant Program	Helps reduce commercial motor vehicle accidents by using commercial vehicle registration systems.	5	2
Safety Data Improvement Grants	Supports states to collect accurate and complete commercial vehicle crash data.	3	1
		Total $298	

Source: GAO analysis of Federal Motor Carrier Safety data. | GAO-15-33

[a]The fiscal year 2013 obligation total for the Motor Carrier Safety Assistance Program Grants includes a $3 million dollar takedown for administrative expenses.

NHTSA

NHTSA collects and reports obligations from the Highway Trust Fund at the grant program level through its Grant Tracking System and Delphi, DOT's accounting system (see table 3). NHTSA obligated almost $600 million in fiscal year 2013 for state grant programs primarily geared towards safety efforts. About two-thirds of this funding was to two grant programs—the State and Community Highway Safety Grant Program and Impaired Driving Countermeasures Grant Program. These grants cover efforts related to data analysis, safety education, pedestrian safety publicity efforts, increasing seat belt and child seat awareness, reducing driving while intoxicated, and other areas. The remainder of NHTSA's program funding was for the Operations and Research account, including impaired driving programs, 911, and driver registration programs. As in previous years, NHTSA's Vehicle Safety

Research program (about $140 million) was funded from the General Fund for fiscal year 2013.[19] NHTSA collects other information at the state level about its grant programs as part of its oversight and monitoring responsibilities in other information systems· For example, some states track types of activities funded with grant awards in NHTSA's Grant Tracking System. In addition, states report, in their annual Highway Safety Plan and annual report, activities funded within each grant program.

Table 3. National Highway Traffic Safety Administration Grant Programs' Obligations from the Highway Trust Fund, Fiscal Year 2013

Program[a]	Program description	Total obligations (dollars in millions)	Percentage
State and Community Highway Safety Grant Programs (formula grants)	Supports state highway safety programs designed to reduce traffic crashes and resulting deaths, injuries and property damage.	$234	40%
Impaired Driving Countermeasures Grant Program	Supports states to adopt and implement programs to reduce driving under the influence of alcohol and drugs.	139	23
Occupant Protection Incentive Grants	Supports states to adopt and implement effective programs to reduce highway deaths and injuries resulting from individuals riding unrestrained or improperly restrained in motor vehicles.	55	9
State Traffic Safety Information System Improvements	Supports improvement of state data to help identify safety priorities.	50	8
Research and Analysis and Highway Safety Research	Funding for research on crash statistics and highway safety.	30	5

Table 3. (Continued)

Program[a]	Program description	Total obligations (dollars in millions)	Percentage
High Visibility Enforcement Program	Funding for the development, production, and use of broadcast and print media in carrying out traffic safety law enforcement campaigns.	29	5
Driving Safety Programs[b]	Supports state programs safety driving programs, by forming partnerships, conducting research, and providing demonstrations.	25	5
Distracted Driving	Supports state efforts to enact laws prohibiting texting while driving and youth cell phone use while driving.	11	2
In-Vehicle Alcohol Detection Device Research	Funding for research on devices that may prevent alcohol-impaired driving.	5	1
Motorcyclist Safety	Support state efforts to adopt motorcyclist safety and road awareness programs.	4	1
Emergency Medical Services[c]	Supports 911 assistance and standardization of emergency medical records.	4	Less than 1
National Driver Register and Driver Licensing	Supports information-gathering about problem drivers and efforts to improve licensing procedures.	4	Less than 1
		Total $592	

Source: GAO analysis of National Highway Traffic Safety Administration data | GAO-15-33

[a]This figures reflect obligated figures only. NHTSA is authorized to reallocate available amounts under the National Priority Safety programs for other authorized purposes. 23 U.S.C. §405(a)(1)(G).

For this reason, there are differences between obligated expenses, unobligated expenses, and NHTSA's reported total budget for most of the grants.

[b]Includes operations and research support for Impaired Driving, Drug Impaired Driving, Safety Countermeasures, National Occupant Protection, and Enforcement Justice Services.

[c]Includes operations and research support for Emergency Medical Service, Enhanced 9-1-1/National 9-1-1 Office, and National Emergency Medical Services Information System.

DOT Administrations Supported a Range of Administrative Expenses with Highway Trust Fund Monies

Within DOT, FHWA, FMCSA, and NHTSA receive Highway Trust Fund monies for administrative expenses such as personnel salaries and benefits and rent.[20] There is no standard definition within DOT of what is considered an administrative expense.

According to DOT officials, MAP-21 and appropriations language establish parameters for the types of activities that can be funded with Highway Trust Fund monies. For example, for FMCSA, administrative funds can be used for, among other things, personnel costs, administrative infrastructure, rent, information technology, programs for research, and such other expenses as may from time to time become necessary to implement statutory mandates of the Administration not funded from other sources.[21]

As shown in table 4, in fiscal year 2013, DOT agencies obligated a total of $752 million for administrative expenses funded from the Highway Trust Fund. This accounted for about 2 percent of Highway Trust Fund obligations by DOT's operating administrations.

MAP-21 also authorized some of FHWA's Highway Trust Fund administrative expense funding to be used for specific programs including the Highway Use Tax Evasion Projects program[22] and On-The-Job Training Support Services program.[23] In fiscal year 2013, FHWA obligated $22 million for these programs.

DOT agencies report information on administrative expenses paid from the Highway Trust Fund in their annual budget requests, which are publicly available.

Table 4. Department of Transportation Activities Funded with Administrative Monies from the Highway Trust Fund, Fiscal Year 2013 (in Millions)

Agency	Fiscal year 2013
Federal Highway Administration	
• General Operating Expenses: Salaries and benefits, travel, transportation, rent, communications and utilities, printing, supplies and materials, equipment, land and structures, and other services	$415
• Other Programs: On-the-Job Training Supportive Services, Disadvantaged Business Enterprise Supportive Services, Highway Use Tax Evasion and others	$22
• Transfers: Appalachian Regional Commission	$2
Total	**$439[a]**
Federal Motor Carriers Administration	
• Programs and Operational Expenses: Salaries and benefits, travel, rent, training, supplies, equipment, contracts, working capital fund, other program costs (such as fleet, border facilities, academy, uniforms)	$196
• Contract Activities: Research and technology, information management, regulatory development, and outreach and education	$50
• Commercial Motor Vehicle Operating Grant	$1
• Motor Carrier Safety Assistance Program Grants takedown	$3
Total	**$250[b]**
National Highway Traffic Safety Administration	
• Operations and Research—Highway Safety Research and Development Administrative Expenses: Salaries and benefits, travel, transportation, rent, communications and utilities, printing, supplies, equipment, unallocated, and other services	$38
• Highway Traffic Safety Grants Administrative Expenses: Salaries and benefits, travel, transportation, rent, communications and utilities, printing, other services, supplies, equipment, and unallocated	$25
Total	**$63**
GRAND TOTAL	**$752 million**

Source: GAO analysis of fiscal year 2013 obligations data from the Federal Highway Administration, Federal Motor Carrier's Administration, and the National Highway Traffic Safety Administration and information in MAP-21. | GAO-15-33

[a]MAP-21 authorized $454,180,326 for fiscal year 2013.

[b]MAP-21 authorized $251,000,000 for fiscal year 2013.

DOT operating administrations have limited flexibility with respect to how Highway Trust Fund monies can be used for administrative expenses and limited flexibility for reallocating full-time equivalents (FTE) funded from the Highway Trust Fund. For example, NHTSA allocates FTEs by program, and no individual NHTSA employee is paid out of both the Highway Trust Fund and the general fund. NHTSA does have some flexibility to fund FTEs from either the Highway Trust Fund or the General Fund with allocations made at the fund level based on the type of work assigned to the employee.[24]

CONCLUSION

Motor fuel taxes that support the Highway Trust Fund are eroding, resulting in fewer resources to fund surface transportation projects and requiring, in recent years, infusions of funding from general revenues. We have reported that continuing to fund the Highway Trust Fund through general revenues may not be sustainable given competing demands and the federal government's fiscal challenges, and that Congress and the Administration need to agree on a long-term plan for funding surface transportation. Given this situation, ensuring that Highway Trust Fund dollars are spent wisely and that its uses are transparent to Congress and the public is important. About $39 billion of FHWA's fiscal year 2013 Highway Trust Fund total obligations of $41 billion were distributed to states through the federal-aid highway program and FHWA is accountable for the efficient and effective use of these funds.

In recent years, FHWA has taken some positive steps to collect and report aggregate spending data for its "major" projects, but does not currently collect and report aggregate spending data for other projects, which represented nearly 88 percent of all fiscal year 2013 federal-aid highway obligations. FHWA could collect and report aggregate spending data for all projects in FMIS since the database already has two existing data fields that could be used to collect this information. According to FHWA officials, collecting this data in FMIS could result in some increased costs to states; however, FHWA does not have an estimate of what the associated costs for tracking this information would be to states. FHWA would have to collect further information on the costs and resources required to make these data fields mandatory and would need to develop data collection procedures to ensure state users are entering and reporting consistent data. FHWA is currently in the process of modernizing its FMIS database system, which could provide FHWA with an opportunity to explore options for further refining FMIS to collect consistent aggregate spending data for all projects or other options for collecting this information. Improving FMIS to allow states to provide project-level data could aid FHWA in its risk-based oversight of federal-aid highway programs by allowing FHWA to more easily draw consistent data for its compliance assessment reviews. In addition, collecting project-level data could assist FHWA in tracking and reporting information to Congress and the public about how the majority of federal funds from the Highway Trust Fund are being used.

Recommendation for Executive Action

To improve transparency and provide Congress and the public greater visibility into the types of highway activities funded with Highway Trust Fund monies, we recommend that the Secretary of Transportation direct the FHWA Administrator to explore the costs, feasibility, and options for collecting and publicly reporting consistent aggregate project-level spending data.

Agency Comments

We provided a draft of this report to DOT for its review and comment. DOT agreed with our recommendation and provided technical comments, which we incorporated as appropriate.

Sincerely yours,
Susan Fleming
Director, Physical Infrastructure Issues

Appendix I: Objective, Scope, and Methodology

The objective of this report was to examine what is known about the types of projects, activities, and federal administrative functions and expenses supported by the Department of Transportation (DOT) using Highway Trust Fund monies in fiscal year 2013.

To identify the types of projects, activities, and administrative expenses that have been undertaken using Highway Trust Fund monies in fiscal year

2013, we obtained and analyzed data from the Federal Highway Administration (FHWA), the Federal Transit Administration (FTA), the National Highway Traffic Safety Administration (NHTSA), and the Federal Motor Carrier Safety Administration (FMCSA) of fiscal year 2013 obligations for all programs and administrative expenses funded with Highway Trust Fund monies. According to DOT, these are the DOT agencies that can directly obligate funds from the Highway Trust Fund. For FHWA data, we obtained and analyzed data from FHWA's Fiscal Management Information System (FMIS) system, which is FHWA's major financial information system for tracking highway projects financed with federal-aid highway program funding. FHWA uses the information entered in FMIS for planning and executing program activities, evaluating program performance, and depicting financial trends and requirements relating to current and future funding. Specifically, we obtained FHWA data for projects with obligated funds in fiscal year 2013 (October 1, 2012, through September 30, 2013). For the purposes of our analysis, we included obligations for all 50 states, District of Columbia, and Puerto Rico, and excluded U.S. territories: American Samoa, Guam, Northern Mariana Islands, and the Virgin Islands from this total. The data set that FHWA provided us, included data for the following data fields: (1) State, (2) Project Number, (3) Fund Source, (4) Recode, (5) Improvement Type (6) Fiscal year 2013 Federal Funds, and (7) Major Project. We analyzed the data to determine the total obligated federal funds for 59 improvement types.[1] We categorized these improvement types into 13 broader GAO categories and determined total federal obligations incurred for each of these categories. (See table 5). About $3.9 million of the entries in the FMIS database did not have an improvement type classification and for the purposes of our analysis, we classified these entries as 'other'. FHWA also provided us with fiscal year 2013 Highway Trust Fund obligations data for programs and administrative expenses not captured in FMIS.

Table 5. GAO Classification of Fiscal Management Information System's Improvement Codes

GAO categories	FMIS improvement code	FMIS improvement code description
Bridges (new construction)	8	Bridge new construction
Bridge rehabilitation and replacement (increased capacity)	10 13	Bridge replacement-added capacity Bridge rehabilitation-added capacity

GAO categories	FMIS improvement code	FMIS improvement code description
Bridge rehabilitation and replacement (no added capacity)	11 14	Bridge replacement-no added capacity Bridge rehabilitation-no added capacity
Bridge improvement	9 12 40 47 48 49	Bridge replacement[a] Bridge rehabilitation Special bridge Bridge preventative maintenance Bridge protection Bridge inspection and related training
Roads (new construction)	1	New construction roadways
Roads - reconstruction (increased capacity)	3	4R-Reconstruction added capacity
Roads - reconstruction (no added capacity)	4	4R-Reconstruction no added capacity
Roads (resurfacing and rehabilitation)	5 6 7	4R-Maintenance resurfacing 4R-Maintenance restoration & rehabilitation 4R-Maintenance relocation
Safety improvement	21 22 38 57	Safety Rail or Highway crossing Safety and education for pedestrians and bicyclists Safety non-infrastructure
Sidewalks and bicycle trails	28	Facilities for pedestrians and bicycles
Other enhancements	29 30 31 32 33 34 35 36 37 39	Acquisition of scenic easements and scenic or historicsites Scenic or historic highway programs Landscaping and other scenic beautification Historic preservation Rehabilitation and operation of historic Transportation buildings, structures, or facilities Preservation of abandoned railway corridors Control and removal of outdoor advertising Archaeological planning & research Mitigation of water pollution due to highway runoff Establishment of transportation museums

Table 5. (Continued)

GAO categories	FMIS improvement code	FMIS improvement code description
Project development activities	15	Preliminary engineering
	16	Right of way
	17	Construction engineering
	18	Planning
	19	Research
	43	Utilities
Other	20	Environmental only
	23	Transit
	24	Traffic management/engineering - HOV
	25	Vehicle weight enforcement program
	26	Ferry boats
	27	Administration
	41	Youth conservation service
	42	Training
	44	Other
	45	Debt service
	50	New tunnel
	51	Tunnel replacement
	52	Tunnel rehabilitation
	53	Tunnel preservation
	54	Tunnel protection
	55	Tunnel inspection and related training
	56	Other asset inspection
	58	Freight
		blank

Source: GAO classification of FHWA FMIS Improvement Codes. | GAO-15-33

[a]We included improvement code 9 (bridge replacement) in the 'bridge improvement' category rather than in the "bridge rehabilitation and replacement with increased capacity" or "bridge rehabilitation and replacement with no added capacity" categories, because FHWA's definition for this code did not specify whether it is used for bridge rehabilitation and replacements projects resulting in increased or no added capacity.

We also reviewed documents from and conducted interviews with FHWA officials to gather information about: (1) the capabilities of FHWA's FMIS database to track project-level data, (2) processes and protocols for tracking and entering project-level data in FMIS, and (3) extent to which FHWA uses FMIS data for project management and risk oversight purposes. To assess the reliability of data collected in FMIS, we reviewed available documentation and interviewed FHWA officials on the procedures used by FHWA and state

Departments of Transportation (state DOT) to enter and verify financial information entered into FMIS. We also conducted electronic testing for duplicate entries and missing values in the data we extracted from FMIS. We found the FMIS data elements we used in our report to be sufficiently reliable for the purposes of reporting federal obligations for fiscal year 2013.

For FTA we requested, obtained, and analyzed FTA data on Highway Trust Fund obligations for all programs in fiscal year 2013. FTA produced these data from its Transportation Electronic Award and Management (TEAM) system and provided us with total federal obligations by program and by 13 categories of activities that GAO reclassified into 9 categories of activities. We did not obtain administrative obligations data from FTA because FTA does not receive funding from the Highway Trust Fund for administrative expenses. Similarly, we requested, obtained, and analyzed NTHSA and FMCSA data on Highway Trust Fund obligations for all programs and administrative expenses during fiscal year 2013. Both agencies produced this data through Delphi, which is DOT's accounting system. We also reviewed publicly available information on FTA, NHTSA, and FMCSA fiscal year 2013 program and administrative obligations from the Highway Trust Fund. We interviewed officials from FTA, NHTSA, FMCSA, and obtained written information about steps taken to ensure the reliability of their data from TEAM and from the Delphi system. We determined that the data were sufficiently reliable for the purposes of this report. We reviewed relevant statutes, regulations, legislation, and other literature including prior GAO reports on Highway Trust Fund authorizations and the types of administrative expenses that can be funded with Highway Trust Fund dollars. We interviewed officials from the DOT, Office of Secretary of Transportation (OST) and the four DOT-operating administrations to obtain additional information on federal obligations from the Highway Trust Fund; the administration's process for tracking and monitoring these obligations; and the flexibility DOT and its operating administrations have to reallocate Highway Trust Fund dollars among offices and other functions. There is no standard definition of administrative expenses. However, for the purposes of our review, administrative expenses were defined as salaries, benefits, travel, and other service contracts. We conducted this performance audit from March 2014 to October 2014 in accordance with generally accepted government auditing standards. Those standards require that we plan and perform the audit to obtain sufficient, appropriate evidence to provide a reasonable basis for our findings and conclusions based on our audit objectives. We believe that the evidence obtained provides a reasonable basis for our findings and conclusions based on our audit objectives.

Appendix II: Detailed Analysis of FHWA's Data on Projects and Other Uses of Highway Trust Fund Monies

In fiscal year 2013, FHWA spent $41 billion from the Highway Trust Fund. Of this amount, $39 billion was apportioned to states through the federal-aid highway program. FHWA also spent about $2 billion of its $41 billion from the Highway Trust Fund for other purposes, including transfers to other DOT and non-DOT federal agencies ($610 million), Federal Lands Transportation Program ($558 million), and research activities ($438 million), among others. In fiscal year 2013, FHWA allocated Highway Trust monies to 28 agencies (8 DOT and 20 non-DOT agencies), including DOT's Federal Railroad Administration and the Department of Interior, among others.[1]

Our analysis of FHWA FMIS data of fiscal year 2013 obligations showed that about 47 percent of total federal obligations went to road improvements, and 17 percent went to bridge improvements. The majority of both road and bridge projects went toward reconstruction, resurfacing, and rehabilitation activities versus new construction. Specifically:

- For roads, about 43 percent was dedicated to resurfacing and rehabilitation of roads with most of the remainder going toward reconstruction with increased or no added capacity.
- For bridges, about 59 percent was dedicated for bridge rehabilitation and replacement with no added capacity and most of the remainder went toward rehabilitation and replacement with increased capacity and other bridge improvements. (See figs. 4 and 5).

In addition, about 29 percent of FHWA federal-aid highway program obligations from the Highway Trust Fund went toward project development, safety, and other improvements. Project development activities include funding for activities such as preliminary engineering activities, construction engineering, research, and other planning activities. Our analysis of this data showed that most of this funding went toward construction engineering (32 percent) and preliminary engineering (29 percent). (See fig. 6.) Safety, enhancements, and other improvements include safety, safety education for pedestrians and bicyclists, and highway crossing activities, among others. Our analysis of this data showed that most of this funding went to safety activities (67 percent). An additional 15 percent went toward facilities for pedestrians and bicycles. (See fig. 7).

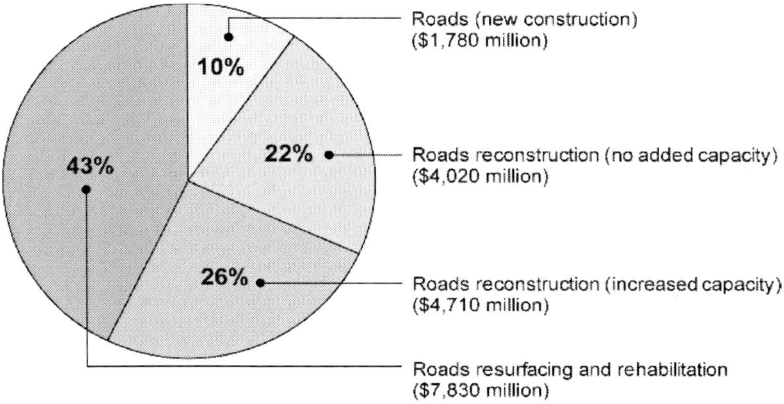

Source: GAO analysis of Federal Highway Administration data. I GAO-15-33.
Note; Figures do not add to 100% due to rounding.

Figure 4. FHWA Fiscal Year 2013 Federal Obligations for Road Projects.

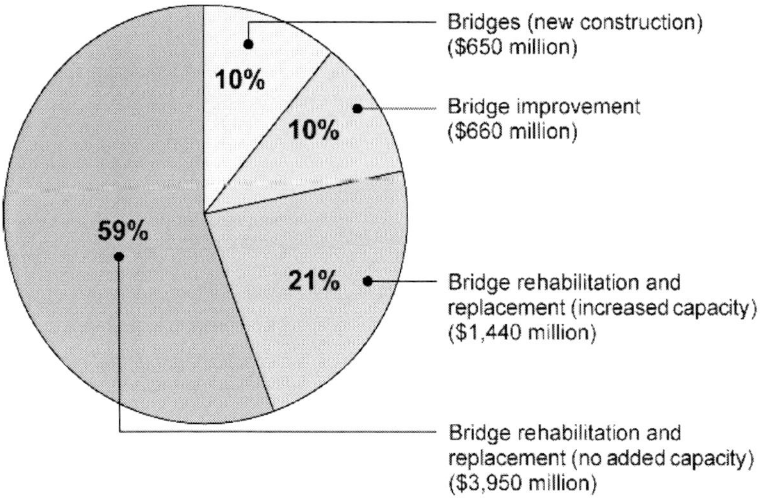

Source: GAO analysis of Federal Highway Administration data. I GAO-15-33.

Figure 5. FHWA Fiscal Year 2013 Federal Obligations for Bridge Projects.

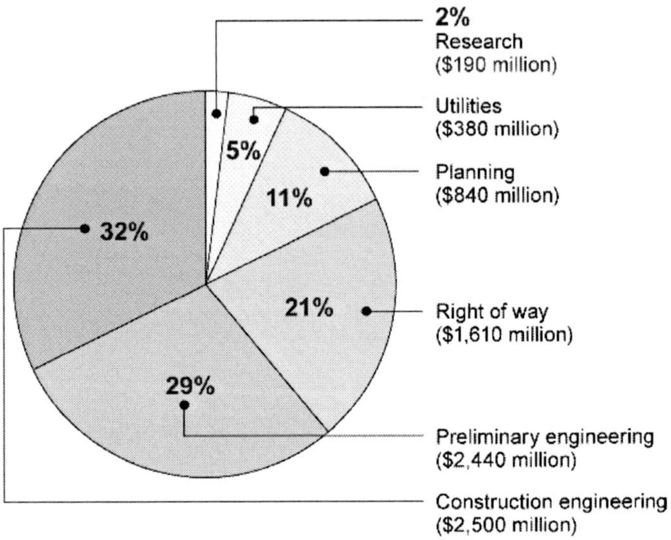

Source: GAO analysis of Federal Highway Administration data. | GAO-15-33.

Figure 6. FHWA Fiscal Year 2013 Federal Obligations for Project Development Activities.

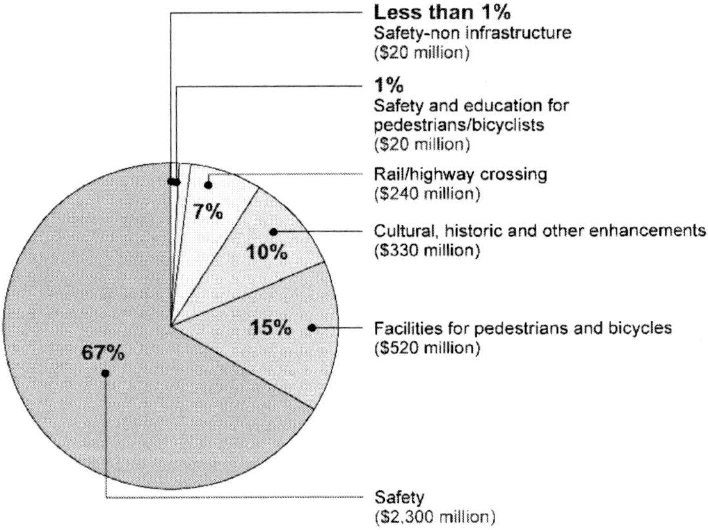

Source: GAO analysis of Federal Highway Administration data. | GAO-15-33.

Figure 7. FHWA Fiscal Year 2013 Federal Obligations for Safety, Enhancements, and Other Improvements.

We also analyzed FHWA FMIS data of projects funded under each of FHWA's five core formula programs. These core programs account for $31 billion (about 76 percent) of the $41 billion that FHWA obligated from the Highway Trust Fund in fiscal year 2013. As discussed below, the types of activities funded under each of these programs varied widely. (See figs. 8-12).

- The National Highway Performance Program (about $17 billion) provides funding for improvements on the National Highway System such as construction, reconstruction, resurfacing, and rehabilitation of National Highway System segments. The majority of this funding was obligated for resurfacing and rehabilitation of roads (21 percent), project development activities (19 percent), and reconstruction of roads to increase capacity (18 percent).
- The Surface Transportation Program (approximately $11 billion) funds the federal share of projects that states and localities may carry out on federal-aid highway , including bridge projects, transit capital projects, and bus facilities. The majority of STP funding was obligated for resurfacing and rehabilitation of roads (26 percent), project development activities (20 percent), and reconstruction of roads with no added capacity (11 percent).
- The Highway Safety Improvement Program (approximately $2 billion) provides funding for activities that reduce the number of crashes, traffic fatalities, and serious injuries on public roads. Most of this funding was obligated for safety improvements (62 percent) and project development activities (20 percent).
- The Congestion Mitigation and Air Quality Improvement Program (about $1 billion) provides funding to state and local governments for transportation projects and programs to help meet the requirements of the Clean Air Act. About 21 percent of this funding was obligated to project development activities, and 24 percent was obligated to other activities, which included activities such as traffic management on high-occupancy vehicle lanes.
- The Transportation Alternatives program (approximately $111 million) provides funding for alternative transportation projects related to surface transportation, such as pedestrian and bicycle trails, community improvement activities, construction, planning, and design of infrastructure related projects and systems that provide safe routes for non-drivers. About 50 percent of this funding was obligated for sidewalks and bicycle trail activities, with most of the remainder

obligated for project development (17 percent) and other (18 percent) activities.

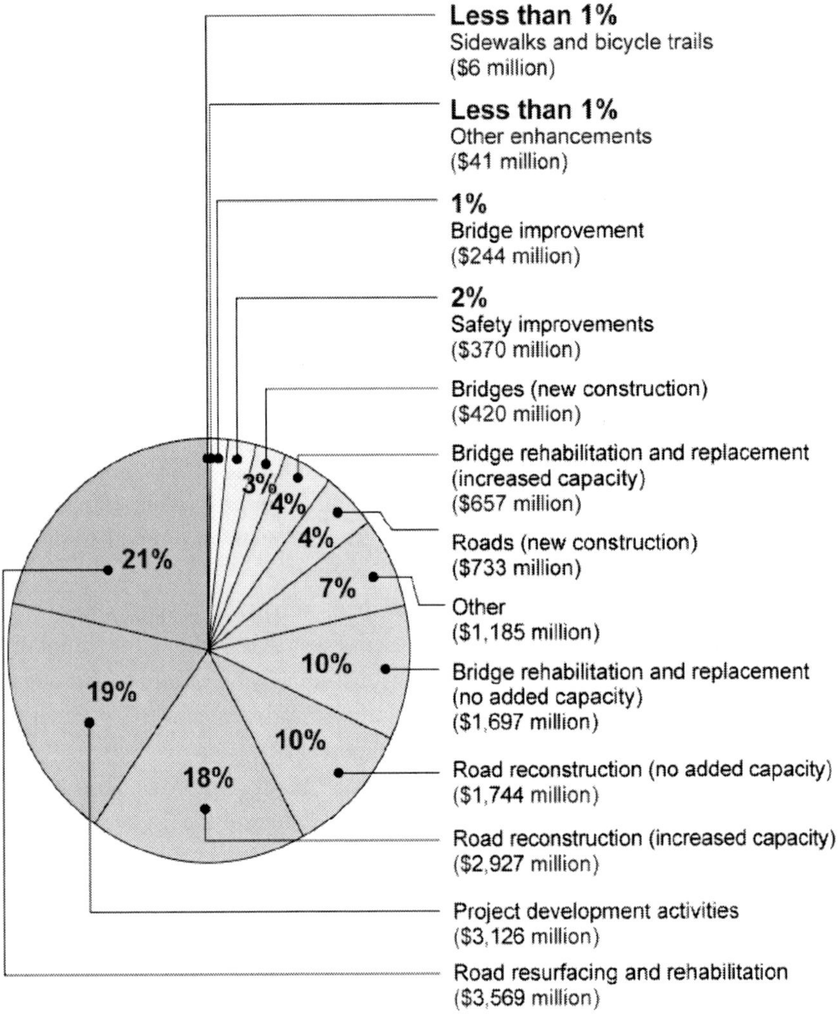

Source: GAO analysis of Federal Highway Administration data. I GAO-15-33.

Figure 8. FHWA Fiscal Year 2013 Federal Obligations for Projects Funded under the National Highway Performance Program.

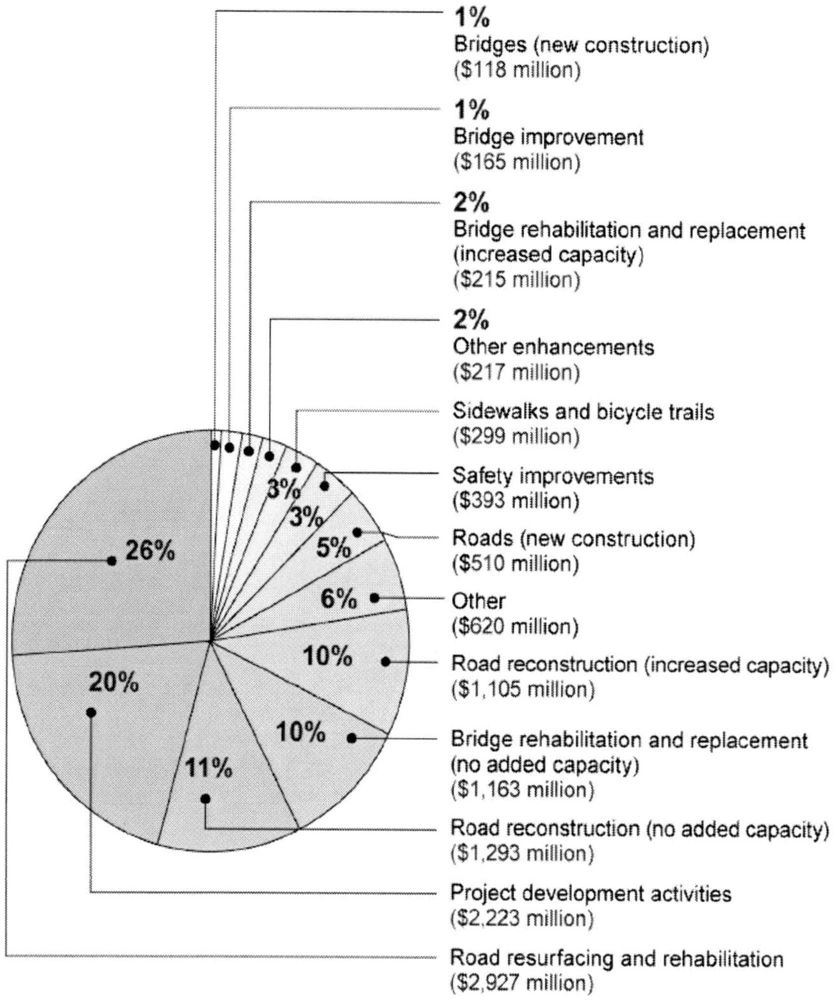

Source: GAO analysis of Federal Highway Administration data. | GAO-15-33.

Figure 9. FHWA Fiscal Year 2013 Federal Obligations for Projects Funded under the Surface Transportation Program.

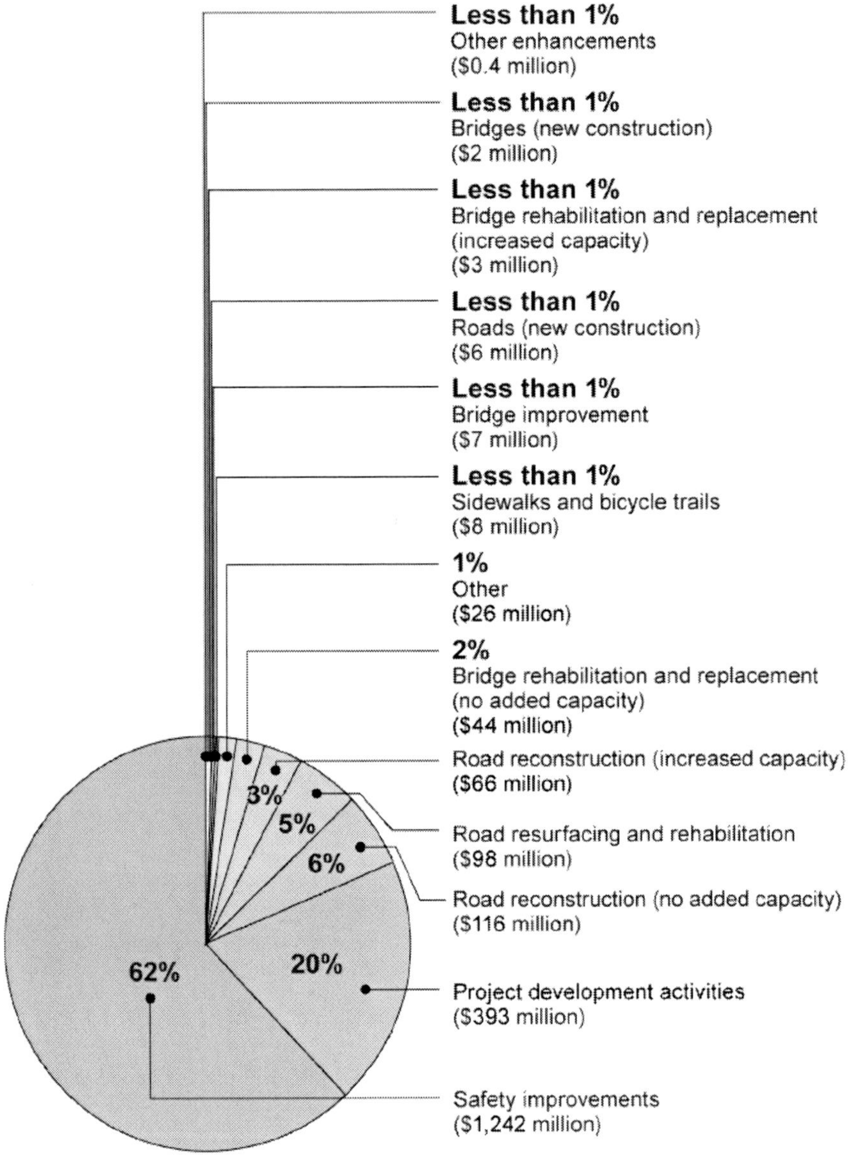

Source: GAO analysis of Federal Highway Administration data. | GAO-15-33.

Figure 10. FHWA Fiscal Year 2013 Federal Obligations for Projects Funded under the Highway Safety Improvement Program.

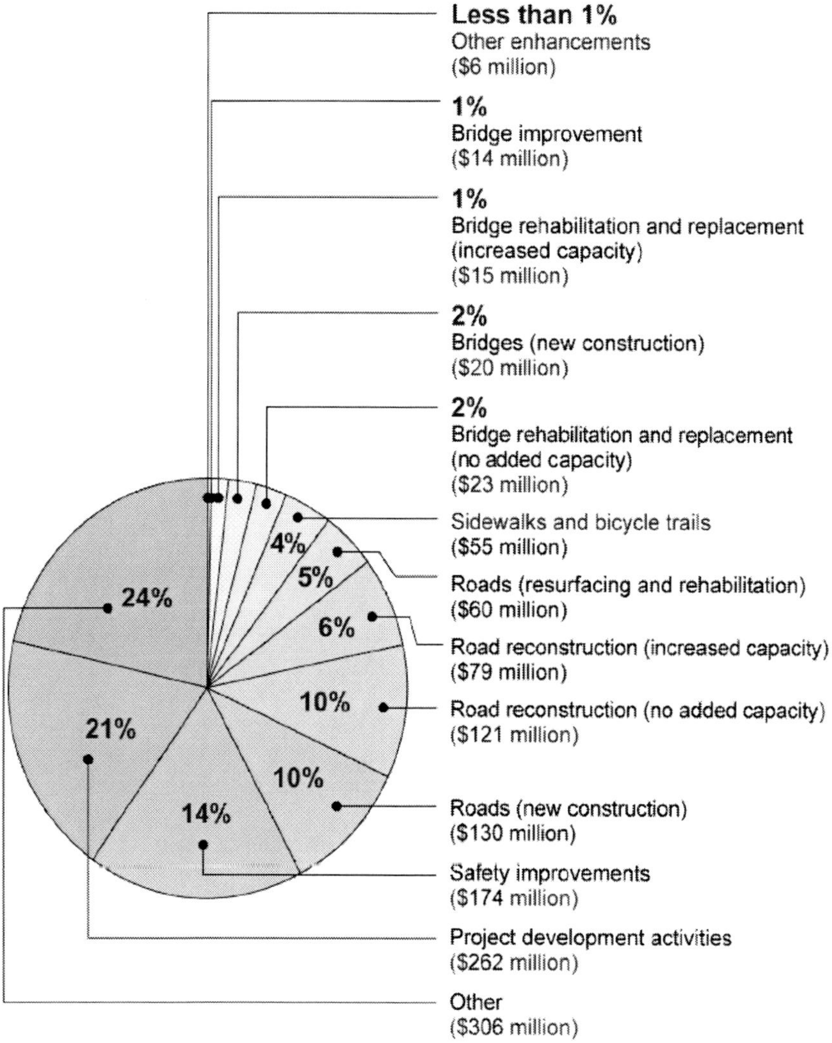

Source: GAO analysis of Federal Highway Administration data. | GAO-15-33.

Figure 11. FHWA Fiscal Year 2013 Federal Obligations for Projects Funded under the Congestion Mitigation and Air Quality Program.

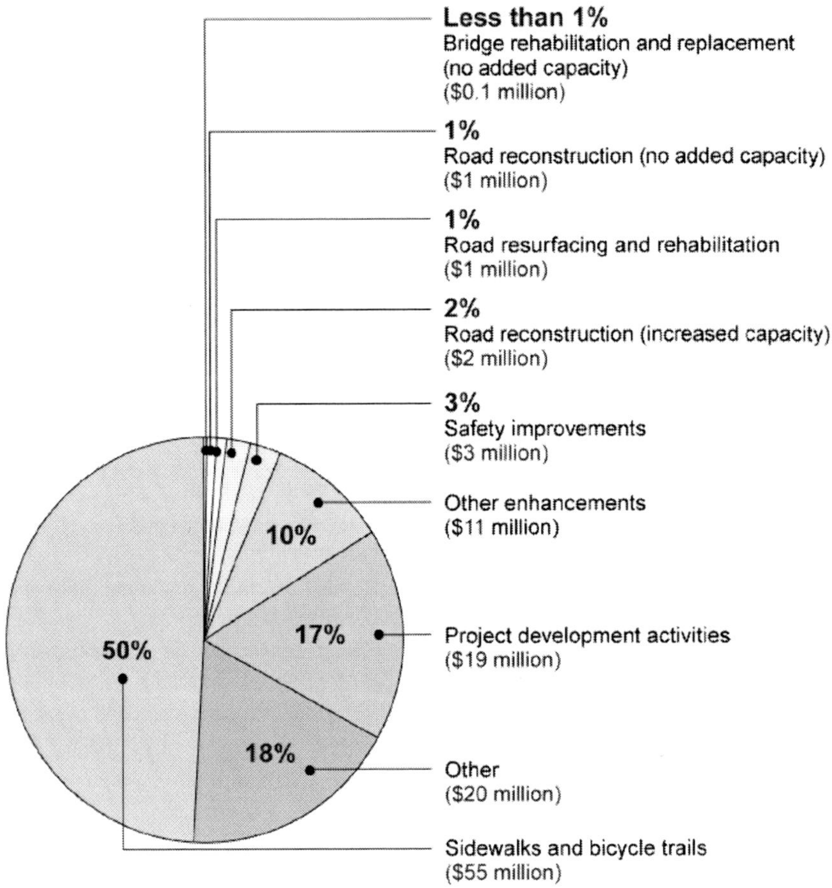

Source: GAO analysis of Federal Highway Administration data. | GAO-15-33.

Figure 12. FHWA Fiscal Year 2013 Federal Obligations for Projects Funded under the Transportation Alternatives Program.

APPENDIX III: ANALYSIS OF FHWA MAJOR PROJECTS BY IMPROVEMENT TYPE

Our analysis of fiscal year 2013 federal-aid highway program obligations for "major" projects showed that over 40 percent of these funds were used for road resurfacing and rehabilitation (24 percent) and project development activities (19 percent). (See fig. 13.) About 6 percent of the funds were used for new construction of roads and bridges, while 7 percent were utilized for safety improvements.

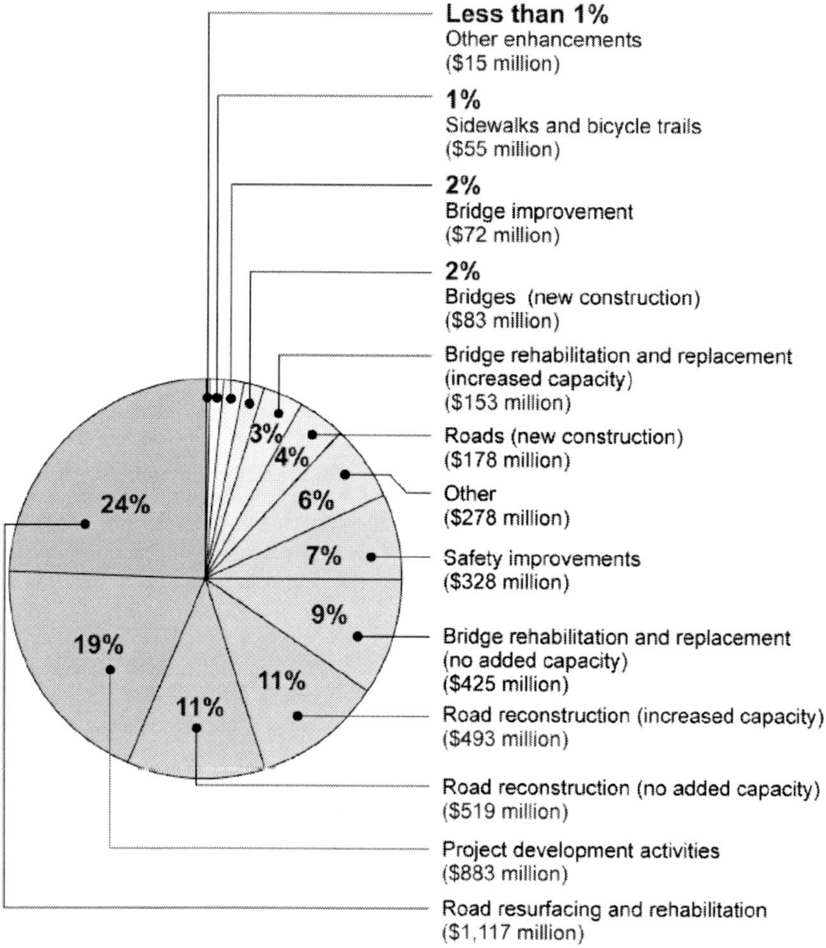

Source: GAO analysis of Federal Highway Administration data. I GAO-15-33.

Note: This analysis includes $4.5 billion in obligations from the Highway Trust Fund and an additional $127 million in obligations from the General Fund in fiscal year 2013 for a total of $4.6 billion in major projects obligations.

Figure 13. FHWA Fiscal Year 2013 Federal Obligations for Major Projects.

End Notes

[1] In addition, $1 billion will be transferred from the Leaking Storage Tank Trust Fund. Highway and Transportation Funding Act of 2014. Pub. L. No. 113-159 (2014).

[2] GAO, *High Risk Series: An Update*, GAO-13-283 (Washington D.C.: Feb. 14, 2013).

[3] Pub. L No. 112-141, 126 Stat. 405 (2012). MAP-21 is the current authorization act for surface transportation programs and will expire at the end of fiscal year 2014. An authorization act establishes or continues federal programs or agencies. MAP-21 provided contract authority over the authorization period for most programs funded from the Highway Trust Fund. Contract authority is a form of budget authority that permits obligations to be incurred in advance of appropriations. Contract authority is unfunded, and a subsequent appropriation is needed to liquidate or pay the spending.

[4] An obligation is a definite commitment that creates a legal liability of the government for payment. Once an obligation is made, the federal government reimburses the states when they submit a voucher for costs incurred on the project.

[5] The Highway Trust Fund also receives revenue attributable to gasoline used by non-highway recreational users, such as snowmobiles, all-terrain vehicles, off-highway motorcycles, off-highway light trucks, and other non-highway motorized recreational vehicles.

[6] The total fuel tax is 18.4 cents per gallon and is split as follows: 15.44 cents to the Highway Account, 2.86 cents to the Mass Transit Account, and 0.1 cent to the Leaking Underground Storage Tank Trust Fund, which is administered by the Environmental Protection Agency. The total diesel fuel tax is 24.4 cents per gallon of which 21.44 cents is dedicated to the Highway Account, 2.86 cents to the Mass Transit Account, and 0.1 cent to the Leaking Underground Storage Tank Trust Fund. Truck related taxes include taxes on tires, truck and trailer sales, and heavy vehicle use taxes.

[7] MAP-21 provides FHWA with fiscal year 2013 authorizations of $41 billion, of which $500 million was authorized to the Projects of National and Regional Significance program. This program did not subsequently receive appropriated funds.

[8] FHWA also administers some older highway programs that previously received appropriations for highway improvements from the General Fund but that have since been eliminated. Projects funded under these programs may still be incurring some obligations. In addition, the Emergency Relief program authorizes FHWA to obligate any funds necessary for the immediate completion of the work. Pub. L. No. 112-141 § 1107.

[9] Generally, the matching-share requirement for federal-aid highway formula grants is 80 percent federal and 20 percent state or local funding. We have previously reported that the funding formula used to apportion funds to states is unsustainable in the longer term because since 2005, every state received as much or more funding for highway programs than they contributed to the Highway Account of the Highway Trust Fund. See GAO, *Highway Trust Fund: Nearly All States Received More Funding Than They Contributed in Highway Taxes Since 2005*, GAO-10-780, (Washington, D.C.: June 30, 2010).

[10] For the purposes of our analysis, we examined federal-aid highway program obligations for the 50 states, District of Columbia, and Puerto Rico. We excluded federal obligations made to American territories, such as Guam, and the Virgin Islands, from our analysis because under MAP-21, American territories receive direct allocations from the Highway Trust Fund rather than apportioned funding by formula. Total federal-aid highway obligations to American territories totaled about $39 million. Puerto Rico also receives direct allocations, but because Puerto Rico is generally treated like a state for various purposes including imposition of penalties and oversight, we kept obligations for Puerto Rico in our analysis.

[11] FHWA tracks obligations for federal-aid highway projects in FMIS and classifies these projects into 59 "improvement types," which indicate the nature of work involved—such as new highway construction, bridge reconstruction—or safety enhancements such as sidewalk and pedestrian safety. For the purposes of our analysis, we reclassified these improvement types into 13 broader categories as described in appendix I.

[12] For the purposes of our report, we use the term "project" to refer to an entire infrastructure improvement project that includes all stages of project development (such as the planning, preliminary design and environmental review, final design and rights-ofway acquisition, and construction stage of a project).

[13] 23 U.S. C § 106(h).

[14] In addition to this amount, $127 million was obligated to major projects from the General Fund in fiscal year 2013.

[15] GAO, *Federal-Aid Highways: FHWA Needs a Comprehensive Approach to Improving Project Oversight*, GAO-05-173 (Washington, D.C.: Jan. 31, 2005).

[16] DOT Office of the Secretary, OIG, *FHWA Needs to Capture Basic Aggregate Cost and Schedule Data to Improve Its Oversight of Federal-Aid Funds,* MH-2005-046 (Washington, D.C.: Feb. 15, 2005).

[17] Some FTA grant programs were amended or were eliminated by MAP-21. For example, a portion of FTA's discretionary Bus and Bus Facilities grant program that provided capital funding to transit providers for bus and bus facilities was eliminated and replaced by a new formula program, the Bus and Bus Facilities Formula Grants. In addition, according to FTA's budget request for fiscal year 2015, the agency is increasing the amount it is requesting from the Highway Trust Fund, by requesting that Capital Investment Grants and the Emergency Relief Program, among others, be funded by the Highway Trust Fund rather than the General Fund.

[18] Most of FMCSA's funding for MCSAP goes to the Basic and Incentive grant programs. Under the Basic and Incentive grant programs, a state-led MCSAP program is eligible to apply for grant funding by submitting a Commercial Vehicle Safety Plan. While Basic grants are focused on initiating safety activities such as roadside inspections, Incentive grants are only provided after the state program has demonstrated safety improvement.

[19] However, for fiscal year 2015, NHTSA requested this program be funded from the Highway Trust Fund.

[20] The Bureau of Transportation Statistics (BTS) also receives Highway Trust Fund monies for administrative expenses and in fiscal year 2013 received about $21 million.

[21] 49 U.S.C. § 31104(i)(2).

[22] 23 U.S.C. §143. The Highway Use Tax Evasion Projects program provides funding to the Internal Revenue Service, other federal agencies and states to carry out intergovernmental enforcement efforts along with training and research to reduce evasion of payment of motor fuel and other highway use taxes.

[23] 23. U.S.C. § 140 (b). The FHWA On-the-Job Training Supportive Services Program provides services to highway construction contractors, highway construction apprentices and trainees to increase the overall effectiveness of a state highway agencies' approved training program and to seek other ways to increase the training opportunities for women, minorities, and disadvantaged individuals.

[24] Pursuant to long-standing appropriations principles, when two appropriations are available for the same purpose, an agency must select which to use, and once it has made an election, the agency must continue to use the same appropriation for that purpose unless the agency, at the beginning of the fiscal year, informs Congress of its intent to change for the next fiscal

year. See, e.g., Comptroller General Decision, Funding for Army Repair Projects, B-272191, Nov. 4, 1997. See also GAO, *Unsubstantiated DOE Travel Payments*, GAO/RCED-96-58R (Washington, D.C.: Dec. 28, 1995).

End Note for Appendix I

[1] FMIS uses improvement types to indicate the main purpose or nature of the work relevant to the database entry.

End Note for Appendix II

[1] FHWA does not classify obligations made to these agencies, the Federal Lands program, and research activities in the same way it does for the federally assisted, state-administered federal-aid highway program because they are not state-apportioned, and as such, these obligations are not included in our analysis of federal-aid highway program obligations.

INDEX

A

access, 16, 21, 23, 25, 27, 49
accident prevention, 43
accounting, 5, 7, 23, 39, 50, 51, 61
administrative functions, vii, 35, 39, 57
agencies, vii, 23, 29, 31, 35, 39, 41, 42, 51, 54, 58, 61, 62, 72, 73, 74
American Recovery and Reinvestment Act, 22, 30
American Recovery and Reinvestment Act of 2009, 22, 30
American Samoa, 58
annual rate, 11
appropriations, 5, 31, 54, 72, 73
assessment, 57
assets, 24
audit, 40, 61
authority, 3, 5, 11, 12, 13, 18, 24, 30, 31, 72
awareness, 51, 53

B

bankruptcy, 28
banks, 23, 25, 31
beautification, 45, 59
beneficiaries, 26
benefits, 14, 15, 17, 19, 25, 26, 27, 30, 37, 54, 55, 61
bond market, 28
bondholders, 22
bonds, 3, 18, 19, 20, 21, 22, 26, 27, 28, 29
borrowers, 19, 21, 23
budgetary resources, 11
businesses, 17, 20, 27
buyer(s), 19, 20, 22

C

campaigns, 53
candidates, 26
capital markets, 23, 28
capital projects, 11, 65
cash, 5, 9, 16, 21, 23, 34
cash flow, 23
Chad, 1
challenges, 30, 38, 56
classification, 45, 58, 60
Clean Air Act, 65
commercial, 43, 50, 51
communication, 49
community, 65
compensation, 23
compliance, 37, 42, 43, 57
conception, 15
Congress, 21, 25, 37, 38, 39, 40, 56, 57, 73
Congressional Budget Office, v, vii, 2, 6, 8, 10, 13, 29, 30, 31, 33, 38
conservation, 60
Consolidated Appropriations Act, 13

construction, 2, 3, 4, 9, 20, 25, 26, 27, 36, 42, 44, 45, 47, 58, 59, 62, 65, 71, 73
consumer price index, 14
corporate average fuel economy, 11
cost, 15, 16, 18, 19, 21, 22, 23, 24, 36, 46, 47, 48
CT, 17
customers, 17

D

data analysis, 51
data collection, 56
data set, 58
database, 37, 39, 56, 58, 60, 74
deaths, 52
debts, 4, 26
deficit, 22
demonstrations, 53
Department of Transportation, vii, 2, 9, 30, 36, 37, 38, 55, 57
deposits, 9
diesel fuel, 2, 3, 6, 11, 14, 72
distribution, 49
District of Columbia, 42, 58, 72
DOT, v, vii, viii, 2, 9, 12, 21, 24, 25, 30, 35, 36, 37, 38, 39, 40, 41, 48, 50, 51, 54, 56, 57, 58, 61, 62, 73
draft, 57
drinking water, 25
drugs, 52

E

earnings, 8, 9
economic downturn, 28
economic efficiency, 14, 15, 17
economic growth, 12
economic performance, 12
education, 42, 51, 55, 59, 62
election, 73
emergency, 53
Emergency Relief Program, 73
employment, 12
enforcement, 16, 50, 60, 73
engineering, 42, 44, 60, 62
Environmental Protection Agency, 31, 72
equipment, 16, 49, 55
equity, 15, 26, 28, 29
ethanol, 5, 14
evidence, 4, 27, 40, 61
exclusion, 29
exercise, 19
expenditures, 7
expertise, 42
external costs, 14

F

fairness, 14
faith, 29
federal agency, 25, 28
federal assistance, 24
federal funds, 5, 13, 25, 30, 31, 37, 42, 43, 48, 57, 58
federal government, 2, 3, 4, 5, 14, 18, 19, 20, 22, 23, 25, 26, 27, 28, 38, 56, 72
Federal Highway Administration, 29, 36, 37, 38, 45, 55, 58, 63, 64, 66, 67, 68, 69, 70, 71
federal law, 42
FHWA, vii, viii, 35, 36, 37, 38, 39, 40, 42, 43, 44, 45, 46, 47, 48, 54, 56, 57, 58, 60, 62, 63, 64, 65, 66, 67, 68, 69, 70, 71, 72, 73, 74
financial, 5, 19, 20, 21, 27, 39, 42, 58, 61
financial condition, 39
flexibility, 56, 61
FMCSA, vii, viii, 35, 36, 37, 38, 39, 40, 43, 44, 48, 50, 54, 58, 61, 73
formula, 29, 41, 43, 52, 65, 72, 73
FTA, vii, viii, 35, 36, 37, 38, 39, 40, 41, 42, 43, 44, 48, 49, 58, 61, 73
fuel consumption, 15
fuel efficiency, 15
fund transfers, 3, 17
funding, vii, 3, 13, 16, 17, 21, 25, 30, 35, 38, 39, 41, 42, 43, 44, 49, 50, 51, 54, 56, 58, 61, 62, 65, 72, 73

funds, 3, 4, 8, 9, 11, 14, 22, 24, 26, 27, 30, 31, 39, 40, 42, 43, 46, 49, 54, 56, 58, 65, 70, 72

G

GAO, vii, viii, 35, 36, 38, 40, 41, 45, 46, 49, 51, 53, 55, 58, 59, 60, 61, 63, 64, 66, 67, 68, 69, 70, 71, 72, 73, 74
goods and services, 17
government spending, 4
governments, 2, 3, 4, 18, 19, 22, 23
grant programs, 43, 44, 48, 49, 50, 51, 73
grants, 5, 23, 24, 25, 27, 28, 29, 31, 39, 41, 42, 43, 48, 50, 51, 52, 54, 72, 73
growth, 47

H

hazardous materials, 43
Highway Trust Fund, 1, iii, v, vii, 2, 3, 5, 6, 7, 8, 9, 10, 11, 13, 14, 15, 16, 17, 30, 33, 34, 35, 36, 37, 38, 39, 40, 41, 42, 43, 44, 45, 48, 49, 50, 51, 52, 54, 55, 56, 57, 61, 62, 65, 71, 72, 73
highways, 2, 3, 4, 5, 12, 13, 14, 15, 16, 17, 18, 27, 30, 42
history, 27
House, 31
House Committee on Transportation and Infrastructure, 31

I

improvements, 2, 16, 39, 44, 62, 65, 71, 72
income, 14, 15, 17, 18, 19, 20, 21, 22, 30, 31, 40
income tax, 17, 19, 20, 21, 22, 30
individuals, 20, 52, 73
industry, 51
inflation, 4, 9, 10, 15, 16, 34, 38
information technology, 51, 54
infrastructure, 2, 4, 12, 13, 17, 19, 20, 21, 22, 23, 25, 26, 30, 31, 43, 44, 47, 54, 59, 65, 73
inspections, 43, 50, 73
interest rates, 18, 23, 24, 28
Internal Revenue Service, 20, 31, 73
investment(s), vii, 12, 13, 24, 26, 27, 28, 30, 35, 39, 50
investors, 20, 22, 23, 25
issues, 2, 31, 43

L

law enforcement, 43, 53
laws, 53
lead, 24, 30
legislation, 5, 7, 40, 61
light, 16, 42, 72
light rail, 42
light trucks, 72
liquidate, 72
loan guarantees, 18, 23, 25, 26
loans, 3, 18, 23, 24, 25, 26, 28, 31
local government, 2, 3, 4, 5, 13, 14, 17, 18, 19, 20, 21, 22, 23, 24, 29, 43, 65
lower prices, 24

M

magnitude, 23
majority, 36, 40, 44, 45, 57, 62, 65
management, 47, 48, 49, 50, 55, 60, 65
mass, 2, 5, 6, 12, 13
materials, 17, 55
media, 53
methodology, 40
Miami, 29
minorities, 73
modernization, 48

N

negative consequences, 12, 14
negative effects, 17

New Starts program, 49
NHTSA, vii, viii, 35, 36, 37, 38, 39, 40, 41, 43, 44, 48, 51, 53, 54, 56, 58, 61, 73

O

Office of Management and Budget, 30
officials, viii, 36, 39, 46, 47, 48, 54, 56, 60, 61
operating costs, 16
operations, 4, 42, 43, 54
opportunities, 73
outreach, 55
oversight, 19, 37, 39, 42, 47, 48, 49, 50, 52, 57, 60, 72
ownership, 28
ownership structure, 28

P

payroll, 30
penalties, 43, 72
personnel costs, 54
policy, 42
policymakers, 24
pollution, 59
population, 47
present value, 23, 31
preservation, 45, 59, 60
President, 21, 22, 25, 31
principles, 28, 29, 73
private sector, 3, 4, 18, 19, 28
program administration, 12
programming, 37, 46
project, 14, 18, 20, 24, 25, 26, 27, 28, 29, 30, 36, 40, 44, 45, 46, 47, 48, 57, 60, 62, 65, 66, 70, 72, 73
protection, 59, 60
public expenditures, 21
public sector, 28
public-private partnerships, 4, 26, 27, 31
Puerto Rico, 42, 58, 72
purchasing power, 14

R

rate of return, 18
reconstruction, 42, 44, 59, 62, 65, 73
recreational, 72
Reform, 23
regulations, 40, 61
rehabilitation, 44, 49, 58, 59, 60, 62, 65, 70
reimburse, 9
reliability, 40, 47, 60, 61
rent, 37, 54, 55
requirements, 41, 42, 43, 46, 47, 58, 65
resources, vii, 4, 14, 22, 24, 27, 35, 46, 48, 56
response, 4, 26
restoration, 59
restrictions, 27
revenue, 2, 4, 5, 12, 14, 24, 25, 26, 38, 40, 72
rights, 44, 73
risk(s), 4, 18, 23, 26, 27, 28, 57, 60
routes, 42, 65
rules, 9, 23, 34
runoff, 59
rural areas, 24, 49

S

safety, 43, 44, 49, 50, 51, 52, 53, 62, 65, 71, 73
schedule delays, 48
school, 25
scope, 19, 40
Secretary of the Treasury, 19, 21, 22
security(s), 22, 49
Senate, 1, 38
services, 14, 17, 43, 55, 73
shortfall, 16, 34
snowmobiles, 72
social costs, 14, 15
society, 14
spending, 2, 3, 4, 5, 7, 8, 10, 11, 12, 13, 14, 17, 23, 27, 29, 30, 34, 36, 38, 39, 42, 44, 45, 46, 56, 57, 72

standardization, 53
state(s), 2, 3, 4, 5, 9, 11, 12, 13, 14, 16, 17, 18, 19, 20, 21, 22, 23, 24, 25, 26, 27, 28, 29, 30, 31, 36, 37, 39, 41, 42, 43, 44, 46, 47, 50, 51, 52, 53, 56, 58, 60, 62, 65, 72, 73, 74
statistics, 52
statutes, 40, 61
structure, 14, 27
subsidy, 19, 20, 22, 23, 24, 25, 31
supervision, 43
suppliers, 17
surface transportation projects, vii, 20, 26, 35, 56

T

target, 47
tax base, 30
tax rates, 17, 38
taxes, 2, 3, 5, 9, 10, 11, 12, 14, 15, 16, 17, 18, 22, 25, 26, 30, 34, 38, 40, 56, 72, 73
taxpayers, 26, 27, 28
technical assistance, 42
technical comments, 36, 57
technology(s), 16, 55
testing, 61
total revenue, 5
tracks, 36, 39, 44, 45, 73
trainees, 73
training, 49, 55, 59, 60, 73
transactions, 29
transparency, 57
transportation, vii, 2, 3, 4, 5, 12, 15, 16, 17, 18, 20, 24, 25, 26, 35, 38, 40, 42, 43, 49, 55, 56, 59, 65, 72
transportation infrastructure, 3, 24, 25
Treasury, 3, 5, 7, 18, 23, 24, 28, 30, 34
treatment, 7, 23, 25, 28
Trust Fund, 1, iii, v, vii, 1, 2, 3, 5, 6, 7, 8, 9, 10, 11, 12, 13, 14, 15, 16, 17, 30, 33, 34, 35, 36, 37, 38, 39, 40, 41, 42, 43, 44, 45, 48, 49, 50, 51, 52, 54, 55, 56, 57, 61, 62, 65, 71, 72, 73

U

U.S. Treasury, 2, 9, 10, 38, 41
United, v, 4, 16, 18, 26, 27, 35, 38
United States, v, 4, 16, 18, 26, 27, 35, 38
urban, 15

V

vehicles, 5, 9, 10, 15, 16, 34, 38, 43, 52, 72
Vitter, 38

W

Washington, 72, 73, 74
wastewater, 25
water, 31, 59

Y

yield, 17, 18, 20